To
Amie
Love

FIGHTING
for MY LIFE

A MEMOIR ABOUT
a MOTHER'S LOSS *and* GRIEF

MIA ST. JOHN
with ELAINE ARADILLAS

A POST HILL PRESS BOOK
ISBN: 978-1-64293-826-5
ISBN (eBook): 978-1-64293-827-2

Cover design by Cody Corcoran
Cover photo by Bobby Quillard

This is a work of nonfiction. All people, locations, events, and situations are portrayed to the best of the author's memory.

Post Hill Press
New York • Nashville
posthillpress.com

Published in the United States of America
1 2 3 4 5 6 7 8 9 10

To Paris, you'll always be my Petit Papillon.

CHAPTER ONE

EVERYONE CALLED HIM PANCHITO. His name was Francisco Bojado and he was a young, up-and-coming fighter with a lot of promise. One morning, he walked into my gym and said, "It's a beautiful day, today. The sun is shining!" Panchito had signed with Main Events, a well-respected group that promotes boxers and matches. He was a friend of Fernando Vargas, a two-time light middleweight champion. Panchito had just started training with my trainers, Eduardo and Roberto Garcia, the much sought-after father-and-son duo. For such a young kid, he possessed the insight of an old soul. He was the kind of guy whose bright smile melted hearts, and he uplifted everyone around him with his fun-loving demeanor. Every time I saw him, he would come in and say the same thing: "It's a beautiful day and the sun is shining."

I was not much of a talker. I preferred to keep to myself and focus on the training drill in front of me. I would smile back and say, "Yeah, it's a beautiful day." I wasn't even sure if I really meant it. It was polite and allowed me to move on.

One day he asked me, "Do you know why I always say that?" I stopped working out to focus on him. I confessed that I didn't. He leaned in as if to tell me a secret. He said the world of boxing was an intense place and a dark world. It's true—it's filled with shadowy deals, foreboding figures, and near-death experiences. "It's so depressing," he said, "that whenever I see the sun shining, I remember the world is a bright place." And as long as the sun was out, he always remembered that.

Those words hung in the gym's stagnant air long after he walked away. And they've travelled with me ever since. He summed up what I had been feeling throughout my career as a fighter. I could never verbalize what it meant to be a fighter until now. I couldn't believe it. Here was an eighteen-year-old boxer whose career was just getting started and he knocked me out with his wisdom. I never saw Panchito after that day. He left for a new gym and went on to represent his country, Mexico, at the Summer Olympics in Australia. I didn't realize the impact his words would have on me, but it was such a relief to know that there was another person in this world who felt the pain and heartache I felt every day in the ring. It's a feeling that's difficult to explain to a person who has never fought for their life. When I step into that ring, I walk into the darkest part of my soul. And when I leave, the dark cloud follows me. There have been moments when the cloud disappears, like on a beautiful, sunny day, or the days I gave birth to my two precious babies, or when I dream about the people I've lost. For those brief periods, I forget my dark world.

It's difficult for me to let go of the darkness that I've carried with me for so long. It may be one of the main reasons I turned to the ring, where I could unload the baggage filled with years of pain I endured throughout my childhood. I felt powerful whenever I took a hit, or better yet, when I gave one. Winning was all I ever wanted, and I chased it for a long time. It's the feeling I live for, and something I can't live without. Losing is a completely different animal. When I lose, I come back stronger and I hit harder, so you won't ever hurt me again. My opponent was a victim of all my dysfunction. My opponent, unknowingly, paid the price for all of my pain.

To know my pain is to learn how I came to be.

I can remember the green, red, and white flags flapping in the wind across the top of the bridge that read "Mexico" each time my family and I crossed the border. I'd sit quietly in the back seat of our car and I'd leave my American world and transport into my mother's. It was hard to believe that a simple bridge connected completely opposite worlds, yet I lived in both. My mother's world began in Juchipila, a small *barrio* in the state of Zacatecas where she was born and raised.

The word Zacatecas comes from the Nahuas word *zacti*, or grass, and *tecatl* means people—*people of the grass*. There was no running water and no electricity. Her house was nothing more than a mud hut. I was two years old, and my sister was almost four. Sometimes, I could almost feel my mother's heart pound when we would cross the border. Even though she had her papers to legally live in the States, the anxiety was palpable. In order to get to Juchipila, it required a brutal four-day train ride deep into an unfamiliar and almost untouched part of the country. It was called Barrio de la Cantera. Rosales was the family name that dominated the town. Everyone knew everybody and were probably related.

We never went for long weekends. When we'd visit, we'd spend long stretches of time there and settle in. Every morning, my sister and I waited outside for the breadbasket lady, who lumbered down the street with a basket of *pan dulce* on her head. It was about six o'clock in the morning and the town's colors would begin to twinkle as the sun began to rise. The sweet bread in her basket came in an array of colors too—pink, coffee, chocolate, and some came dotted with vanilla sprinkles. I can still smell the pastries. When we'd reach for our favorite one, unsurprisingly, ants trailed across the top. We didn't care. We brushed them off and ate our sweet bites of heaven. We weren't picky because we never knew when we'd see treats like this again. The nearest *mercado*, or supermarket, required a *burro* ride into the city, which rarely happened. If we didn't get pan dulce, we devoured delicious guava we'd picked from the trees. Before we ate them, we'd have to pick out the worms nestled inside. Mexico was a hard life, but we never complained.

My mother grew up with orange, lime, and lemon trees. She often described the oranges becoming so ripe that they looked gold in the sunlight. She thought it was magic, and so did I. The barrio was filled with *obeliscos romero* flowers, and a *guayacan* tree that bloomed with bright yellow flowers that smelled like summer. The plant would climb across the trees like a winding rope. My mother would swing from them and imagine she was in a jungle only found in fairy tales. It was during these moments that she admitted she felt incredibly alone, wondering if there was more beyond her barrio.

My sister and I would play in the sugar cane fields while the women walked to the nearby river to wash the clothes and dishes. Everything was lush and green in Juchipila. The days were beautiful, and the nights were unforgettable. In the neighboring city, there were carnivals blanketed with countless strings of lights, but in the barrio, there were bonfires. The fire would get so high, I was sure the flames could touch the stars. We'd laugh and dance while drinking our Cokes, as the grown-ups sat around drinking their beer and wine. Once when we were visiting, I walked into a store and heard Neil Diamond's "Cracklin' Rosie" in Spanish. It became my favorite song, and I learned every word in Spanish. It would be many years later that I'd finally learn that Neil Diamond wasn't Mexican, and that he was Jewish.

For the longest time, I didn't know much about other religions beyond Catholicism. Everyone I knew was Catholic. As children, we were taught to fear God, and the churches used to scare my sister. Whenever you walked inside, you're confronted with a looming statue of Jesus nailed to the cross, fake blood dripping from his crown of thorns, and anguish washed across his face. I'm surprised it lures anyone to church, but it had such an impact on my sister that she refuses to go near them to this day. My sister was the older, wiser one. She always questioned the world, our society, and its rules. "How do we even know there is a God?" she would ask. I think she was born an atheist.

Before my sister and I were born, my mother Maria Elena Socorro Rosales grew up in Juchipila. She was the oldest of her siblings. Her mother left for Mexicali, which was closer to the border, so she could make more money to send home. Once my mother's siblings were old enough to take care of themselves, she left to join her mother. She had a desire to find out if there was indeed a bigger world.

My father, who lived in San Diego, would drive two hours to visit my mother's restaurant. He was more than six feet tall and appeared larger than life. He'd walk through the door like an extra from a John Wayne movie. He'd saunter to his favorite table with all eyes on him, including my mother's. He'd order a plate of *huevos rancheros*, a popular style of scrambled eggs with salsa, and chat with my mom.

I don't know much about my father's family history, but this is what I do know. He was born in Washington, DC, to Gerald and Noel Richardson. My grandfather, who I never knew, supposedly left his family when my father was very young. My grandmother, who I met only a few times, relinquished custody of her three children. The kids were separated and sent to Catholic orphanages, which my father continually ran away from and eventually escaped. By the time he was nine years old, he had already learned to fend for himself. I heard stories that he began drinking before he was ten, and often got into trouble. At the age of sixteen, he joined the US Navy. I wasn't very close to him, and since he was gone the majority of my life, I never learned much about him.

When my father visited my mother, she would practice her English with him, and she eventually asked him out. My mother was a feminist before anyone knew what it meant. She just knew what she wanted and went for it. Eight months later, against my grandmother's wishes, they were married in secret. My grandmother, a wise Indian woman, could see what my mother couldn't. She knew the pain and heartache that man would inevitably cause her daughter. A year later, my mother moved to the United States with my father.

My mother had never stepped on American soil before. She was in awe as she embarked on her new adventure. The country was so clean and modern. She discovered hamburgers and French fries, the ultimate American meal. It was the '60s in Southern California and everything buzzed with electricity, like someone had plugged in the city and turned on the neon lights. There were towering buildings everywhere and everyone who walked among them was dressed to impress with their pressed suits and golden baubles draped around their neck and wrists. She was a fairy princess who married her Prince Charming and was swept away to an electric wonderland.

Before she got married, she was a poor, uneducated Mexican woman who couldn't speak English. But as reality began to slowly set in, she realized her prince wasn't much better off. He was poor and working as an airline mechanic, but he was going to college, where he studied engineering. My parents planted themselves in Palo Alto, California, just outside the city of San Francisco. My sister was born in 1965 and they named her Leslie Marie. My sister was born with light skin and light brown hair just like our father. She looked nothing like our mother, whose prominent Aztec features meant toasted, dark skin and jet-black hair. My sister not only resembled my father, but also inherited his personality and characteristics. She got his horrible eyesight, his introverted nature, but also his smarts. My sister and father had this incredible, natural intelligence that never ceased to amaze me. But unlike my father, she's insightful, compassionate, and tolerant. She's also kind and rarely passes judgment on anyone. She possessed strength and could be very opinionated, which resulted in her and my father often butting heads. There were times they could debate for hours. I never chimed in because I never had any interest in whatever they were discussing, plus I never had enough knowledge on the subjects they discussed.

Less than two years later, in 1967, I was born at San Mateo County Hospital and they named me Maria Elena. Unlike my sister, I was born with dark skin and jet-black hair, just like my mother. She used to call me her little *negrita*, which in Spanish is a *cariño*, or a loving term. But it just made me self-conscious. I had large lips and a big nose to go with it. I was without a doubt my mother's daughter and our personalities definitely matched too. I was very temperamental and fiercely independent. I always wanted to do things on my own without help from anyone. This particular trait drove my father crazy. I wasn't as naturally intelligent as my sister. Throughout school, I struggled to make Cs and Ds. No one ever taught me how to study, but luckily, like my sister, I loved to read. My problem was that I could never retain the information for long. My sister, on the other hand, could recite the Declaration of Independence if she had to.

We were constantly on the move. I was a shy kid who stayed close to my sister. After my father graduated from college, we moved wherever his job took us. Paradise didn't last long for my mother. She had two children and still no money. Her husband would patronize the bars every night after work. There were numerous occasions that my mother dragged me along as she stormed into the go-go bars searching for my drunken father.

She told me life was never as idyllic as she thought it was in the beginning, she says she just didn't want to see it. She had always dreamed of coming to America and living amongst the rich. She wanted the American Dream that she'd heard so much about. Living with an alcoholic in an apartment with barely enough money for food was not the dream she wanted. My mother, however, had her own way of dealing with her situation. She was a compulsive cleaner. As a child, I have very few memories of my mother. They mostly consist of images of her with her hair tied back, cleaning every nook and cranny of our shoebox apartment, and the smell of Pine-Sol permeating the air. I guess it was her way of forgetting her miserable life.

As much as I loved my mother, she had her faults. Being from another country and unable to speak the language was especially difficult for her. Cleaning was her way of not having to interact with her children, of not having to interact with anything. In the frontera, on the farms, kids were simply a product of life. There wasn't anyone around to speak to women about birth control or family planning. Once children were born, as soon as they could walk, they helped their parents on the farms and in the fields. Children became workers. They grew up and had children of their own who also became workers. And on and on. But this didn't mean they didn't have dreams. Even in America, my mother wasn't any different from the women raised in the barrio. Instead of going to the Gymboree or scheduling mother-and-child play dates, we worked in the house and cleaned with my mom. But we were not your typical Mexican children. We were not grateful just to have food on the table or accept our place in life as workers. We were from America and we wanted to do what all of the other American children were doing—playing, playing, and more playing. I wanted to sing and dance, but my mother never let me take lessons. She told me that I would never need those skills in life. There were no ballet classes or even a Girl Scout troop.

My mother didn't speak English, but she tried, so we spoke a sort of Spanglish—a terrible mix of Spanish and English. I grew up feeling like I didn't really belong to either group. My mother wanted us to blend into the white population around us. But it was never going to happen, especially for me. I never felt like a part of white America. The girls around me had names like Jenny and Melanie with their blonde ponytails bopping to their favorite hits on the radio. I grew more isolated. In fact, I felt like an outcast. Meanwhile, I never felt fully Mexican either because I couldn't fluently speak the language. The barrier prevented me from fully connecting with my own mother. If you and your mother don't speak the same language, how can you communicate on a deeper level? I connected with her spiritually and emotionally, but I could never fully express myself. And she couldn't either. There was always a gap between us whenever we tried to meet each other in the middle. We viewed the world through different lenses. I resented her for not making me a part of her world, leaving me in a world where I couldn't relate to anyone.

Most of the places we lived while growing up were in white, middle America, where Mexicans stayed with Mexicans and whites stayed with whites. There wasn't any room for the ones in the middle. I hated being in my own skin. To the Anglos, I was a poor Mexican girl, and to the Mexicans, I was a disgrace. My mother believed that not only was the glass never half full, but it always had a hole in it. We were never good enough, which included me. I now know she felt this deep inside of herself: she wasn't good enough and those feelings of self-hatred inevitably trickled down to her children. My mother deserved better than this life offered her, but she didn't believe it for herself. What other explanation is there for staying with a cheating alcoholic for more than twenty years? My mother was often an angry person, and rarely did I ever see her happy, laughing, or smiling. She'd ask, "What is there to be happy about?" A lot of Mexican women like my mother believed they were helping their children when they cut them down, believed it would prevent the disappointment that came with striving for more.

My siblings and I eventually clamored for more but not without our own battles of dysfunction. I believe if you keep tearing down a child's self-esteem, they will do one of two things: 1) succumb to the negative thoughts, or 2) get angry and fight to prove everyone wrong. I chose the latter, that's the personality I have. I'm stubborn and independent, sometimes to a fault, and I'm constantly trying to prove people wrong. If you say I can't, I will. And that's what I did. When my parents told me I was stupid, a whore, and good for nothing, I rebelled. But it wasn't immediate. There was a fire growing inside of me. At first, I let those descriptions define me. It would take time before I rebelled to prove them all wrong.

CHAPTER TWO

WHEN I WAS A TODDLER, MY FAMILY AND I WOULD TRAVEL BACK AND FORTH BETWEEN OUR HOME IN SOUTHERN CALIFORNIA AND MY MOTHER'S HOME IN MEXICO. When I was four, my grandmother passed away from pneumonia. I saw her for the last time in a rundown Mexicali hospital. I didn't fully understand what was happening, but I have two vivid memories from that time. I remember running toward her and jumping on her bed, only to get tangled in her IV and distressing everyone. And the funeral. My aunt screamed violently into the coffin and demanded that her mother wake up. Her long, black hair that covered her face was soaked in tears, and she pounded her fists against the coffin. I looked up at my mother and she stood there motionless, without any expression. Her reaction confused me. She didn't cry or even appear sad. Later, she told me she wasn't sad because she believed her mother was in a better place. She says my grandmother suffered throughout her life, saving her drunk sons from jails and bars, and working hard to protect her family. Even though she remained stoic in public, many times I heard my mother cry in private. It would be years before I understood the layers of emotions that came with grief.

After the funeral, we left Mexicali for Juchipila, where my mother was born and raised. We spent a few months surrounded by family, but it was time to leave. I was going to start kindergarten in Pompton Lakes, New Jersey. Shortly afterward, we relocated to Phoenix, Arizona, and then to Houston, Texas—all before I started the first grade. It was 1974 and Steve Miller had a hit called "The Joker," a song that I still love. Twister was a game at every party. *The Six Million Dollar Man* was a TV hit, and beads and long hair were a must. I remember Houston fondly except for the cockroaches. They came in all sizes and they were everywhere. There was nothing you could do to get rid of them. But this was also the year my brother was born.

He was named Duncan like my father. My brother looked a lot like my sister. He was light skinned with brown hair and hazel eyes. Oddly, he didn't look like my mom or my dad. My father wasn't around much after my brother was born. My parents' problems were growing and little attention was paid to my brother. I took him under my wing and never let him go unnoticed, especially when I was around. If I wasn't trying to teach him football, then I was helping him with his schoolwork. My brother was different than my sister and I, he was funny, charismatic, outgoing, and always saw the glass half full. He still does.

I was almost seven when I learned how to fight. My father enrolled my sister and I into Tae Kwon Do, a sport that he adored. My father was not affectionate, and he definitely never hugged me, but he showed us what he loved. My dad introduced us to fishing and camping, his hobbies that I came to love. As we moved from city to city, he made sure to show us the Grand Canyon, Niagara Falls, Mount Rushmore, the Washington Monument, and so many other places. He appreciated nature and so did I. I can't say that I loved the martial arts as much as he did, but I was very good at it.

As quickly as we settled in, it was time to move. I started second grade at Nodland Elementary School in Sioux City, Iowa. Middle America and I did not get along. The kids at school were shocked at my appearance. They questioned my skin color, my oversized lips, and my downturned eyes. They didn't know what to make of me. They called me everything from the N-word to a wetback.

One day, I was playing in the schoolyard and the kids backed me up against a wall, taunting me and throwing rocks until I fell to the ground, crying and wetting my pants. A teacher stopped the incident and called my mother to come pick me up. I was humiliated. For the first time in my life, I was mad at my mother for being Mexican. I wanted to scrape my skin off and cut off all of my ethnic features. I wore a clothespin on my nose every night hoping it would shrink. I used peroxide on my face to lighten my skin. Before this, my mom put my hair up in *trenzas*, or braids. She dressed me in colorful, frilly clothes like the Mexican girls always wore back home. My mother took pride in how we looked. But I didn't want to look Mexican anymore, I wanted to be white like everyone else.

I refused to wear anything that looked Mexican. It didn't help that every time my mother saw someone that looked remotely Latino, she'd corner them and ask if they spoke Spanish. She was desperate to speak to anyone that spoke her language. This mortified me and my sister. Now, I look back with so much sadness, knowing how alone she must have felt. Her desire for a better life was so strong that she sacrificed a lot of her own happiness.

A few years later, in 1977, my father moved us to a small town in the state of Washington. He worked at the Trojan Nuclear Power Plant located in Rainier, Oregon. The town we lived in was just across the border into

Washington, a town called Carrolls. Our home was just across the state border. The house sat on a hill, miles away from any city. It overlooked the Columbia River where you could see the power plant. At night, I would stare through the evergreen trees at the glowing lights that surrounded the plant. There was no better place to be, I thought.

Our ranch-style home was a dream for my family because up until then, we didn't have money. It felt like we'd won the jackpot. My father built us a swing, a basketball court, and a little makeshift softball field on the side of the house. The previous owner left us two dogs—a dachshund named Belji for my sister, and a lab named Buck for me. Buck and I would go on long hikes throughout the hills, stopping along the way to nibble on wild blackberries. It rained a lot, but after a while, I grew to enjoy it. Everything was so green and when the sun shined, it glistened like lush paradise.

I started the fourth grade at Carrolls Elementary School, which looked like it belonged in a storybook. It sat on top of another hill, away from the rest of the world, just like everything else in Carrolls. On my first day of school, the teacher introduced me to the class as "our new student from Iowa." I quickly became the teacher's pet. I was shy but I made good grades. I was always willing to please. The kids, of course, resented me for this.

As one of the few kids of color in the school, I suffered the same ridicule as I did in Iowa, only worse, because my new school was a fraction of the size of Sioux City and the taunting was amplified. In the fifth grade, I'd finally had enough. I was playing on the monkey bars when a petite, blonde, blue-eyed girl named Stephanie began chanting the N-word at me. My blood was boiling and my head was spinning. For the first time, I fought back. I grabbed the girl's head and slammed it against the bars until she slid down into the sand, barely conscious. The kids came running, and started screaming, "Go back to Mexico!" I heard one of them say, "Why don't you wipe the dirt off your face!" Stephanie was shaken up, but she turned out fine. Meanwhile, I felt powerful. The next day, to my surprise, everyone smiled and said hi to me in the hall. I would never let anyone call me names again. But to be honest, a part of me felt ill that it had come to that. I never liked hurting anyone.

That same year, I joined the boys' basketball team because the girls' team was hopeless. I once tried to be a cheerleader, but it lasted for a day. I wanted to be a part of the action, not dressed in a miniskirt with pom-poms. I was a tomboy as a child. I was sometimes teased for looking like a boy. It didn't help when I cut my beautiful long black hair to a short bowl cut like Dorothy Hamill. I wore wide-leg jeans and flannel shirts, which I often paired with T-shirts that read "Disco Fever" or were emblazoned with a giant marijuana leaf across my chest. I was only ten and hadn't experimented with drugs, but it was cool. It was the '70s and we lived in Washington, where grunge existed long before anyone ever called it that.

I started my seventh grade year at Coweeman Middle School. I was twelve years old and vowed to make it my most memorable year. It seemed like overnight that I blossomed. My hair grew out and I started wearing makeup, glossy lip gloss, and lots of rouge. I wore tight shirts, and tighter wide-legged jeans with straw platform heels. I was asked to go out with so many guys, I didn't know who to pick, so I chose all of them. This was not a wise choice because I developed quite the reputation. Transforming from the ugly duckling to an attractive swan was overwhelming.

Every Friday night, my sister and I went to Skate World for disco skate night. We would spend hours getting ready for the night. We'd skate to songs like "My Sharona," "Le Freak," and "Any Way You Want It." My sister and I dressed identically, usually satin jackets and San Francisco jeans. I wish this time in my life never ended. I had my first boyfriend, who I met every Friday. He was blonde and fair skinned, and the first boy I ever kissed. A slow song came on and everyone coupled up. We skated with our arms around each other and then he kissed me. It was perfect. I dreamed about that night for days afterward. He ended up dumping me after a month, and I pined away for him for years.

Meanwhile, at home, it had been blissful without my father, who'd been traveling around the world for his job. I'd gone through puberty, had a boyfriend, and left behind my ugly duckling status when he returned for a short time from Hawaii, where he had been living and working at a power plant. My peaceful world suddenly turned upside down. My father couldn't handle the change—we had grown up without him. One night, in a drunken rage, he banned me from phone calls, makeup, and boys. It was one thing for my mom to hit us and yell, but for a stranger to do it? He was a stranger to us. He had no right to tell us what to do. I couldn't believe he thought he could waltz into our lives and play father for the few days he was home. Just like at school, I refused to endure his attacks and yelled back. I instantly saw the rage in his eyes that I'd spent a lifetime avoiding. He chased me around the living room, and I ran for my life.

My father was huge and had the face of a drill sergeant. My sister and I nicknamed him KK for King Kong. I knew that if he caught me, I was dead. My sister also knew this and intervened. She yelled at him and brought the attention to herself. I watched helplessly as she paid dearly for my actions. He pinned her against the wall and whipped her legs with his belt, but she refused to cry, so he punched her in the face. She didn't flinch and grew defiant. I was scared. As he continued to hit her, she didn't move or make a sound. She refused to give him the satisfaction that he affected her, and I watched her spirit float away.

It took weeks for my sister's bruises to fade away. I hated him and I wanted him to disappear. I found ways to deal with his presence, namely his liquor cabinet. I remember being alone one night while my parents were getting blitzed somewhere. I reached into the cabinet and helped myself to a bottle of Galliano and creme de cacao. I was twelve years old. Alcohol gave me a good feeling. I felt the pain in my soul go numb, all the feelings of being worthless and not feeling good about myself diminished. I didn't feel like a poor Mexican girl anymore. I didn't feel anything. I never felt comfortable in my own skin. I never liked who I was, and I always wanted to be someone else. It was as though everyone around me knew my family was dysfunctional. I hated myself and the dark cloud that surrounded our home. By the time my parents returned, they were too drunk to notice. I drowned my pain with alcohol, and I never wanted to be sober again.

Believe it or not, I loved my father. I always imagined that without the alcohol, he might be a good person, but he just couldn't stop drinking no matter how hard my mother tried to get him to stop. At some point, my father started using cocaine because the alcohol depressed him so much. He used coke to bring him up and alcohol to bring him down. I watched him spiral downward into the ultimate hell. I had no idea then that it was only a matter of time before I entered that darkness myself. It was inevitable.

After a difficult night, an argument erupted between my parents. My father had a gun collection, and he'd often point his rifle at one of us and threaten to shoot us. On this particular night, he terrorized my mother. He grabbed her by the hair, pointed the gun at her head, and threatened to shoot her. This time, I thought he was going to pull the trigger. My sister and I begged him to stop and for some reason, he did. Afterward, I wanted to kill him. If I could have gotten away with it, I would have. I prayed for God to free me from this monster.

Instead, he took us with him to Hawaii for a two-week visit. I tried to spend as little time as possible with him, so I befriended some locals who introduced me to weed. It was the first time I had gotten high and it was the best feeling I ever felt. I spent years chasing that same high, but I never felt that good again. It felt like someone lifted me into the air and I soared through the sky like a bird—happy and free from all my worries. My sister was horrified when she caught me smoking a joint at a party. She told me she was disappointed. My father said he never moved us to Hawaii because the drug use was rampant. We returned to Washington without my father, but our break wouldn't be long.

He came home to tell us that we were moving. I was angry and refused to accept this. I had grown attached to this emerald paradise where I had friends and a new boyfriend. It was the first place I finally felt accepted. I had been there for four years, which is a lifetime in teen years. I wanted to spend the rest of my childhood there. It was the only stability I had ever known and now it was being ripped from me.

I prayed for God to intervene. Instead, in June of 1980, our beautiful mountain home was packed. I cried so hard that my stomach hurt. I said goodbye to the trees that I loved so much, my Columbia River that ran across my front yard, the Trojan Power Plant and its beautiful lights—I said goodbye to all of it. I looked out the rearview window as our station wagon slowly made its way down our mile-long driveway. As the rain hit the window of the car, my tears streamed even harder.

My father angrily turned around and yelled, "If you don't stop crying, I'm going to break your nose."

I looked out the window and swore that I would never allow myself to love something this much again.

My sister looked at me and gave the KK hand signal in sign language. It was our way of saying to each other, in private, "Don't worry, things will be okay."

My sister was the other stability in my life. When everything around me changed, she was always there. I think that's why today I have such a hard time with change. I want everything to stay the same, but it never does. The worst part about this particular change was moving to Boise, Idaho, an area known for its history of racism.

We arrived in Boise and as we waited at a stoplight, a tumbleweed passed in front of us just like in the old westerns on television. My sister and I looked at each other in disbelief. We were back in the Midwest.

I entered eighth grade wearing wide-legged jeans, high heels, and feathered hair, while everyone else was wearing polo shirts and 501s with short, clean-cut hair. I was definitely a misfit. I wanted to be high or drunk, so I wouldn't have to deal with the pain in my heart. I immediately hooked up with the school's drug users and searched for drugs every day. I needed to be high. It was my only escape. The students tortured me with the name-calling: spic, beaner, wetback. I demanded respect and threatened anyone who got in my way. Not only was I labeled a poor Mexican girl, but a crazy one. The kids thought I had a screw loose, and maybe I did.

Shortly after we moved to Idaho, my father left my mother for another woman. I came home from school and he was drunk on the couch. Whenever he was home before me, I'd hold my breath and sneak into my room, hoping he wouldn't notice. Shortly afterward, I heard my mother's car in the driveway. I held my breath again while I waited for her to come inside and the yelling to start. It never happened. Instead, I heard hushed voices and whispers for the rest of the night. The next day, he was gone. Looking back, I realize it was his plan the entire time. He had to get us out of the house in Washington in order to get possession of it in court. He left my mother with no money, no job, unable to speak English, and three children to care for. It turned out he'd been with this woman for quite some time. Now we knew why he spent so many years away from home. I didn't see him again for nearly a decade. At the time, I didn't care.

After he left, we relied on the Salvation Army and the Mormon church for help. Religion was one of the few comforts for my mother. We left the Catholic church for Jehovah's Witness. My mother constantly searched for a higher power to save her from the pain in her own life. We bounced around from church to church, searching for "the truth." Even though we were Jehovah's Witnesses, we still celebrated the forbidden holidays—birthdays, Christmas, and Easter. I did sit out reciting the Pledge of Allegiance at school. I don't think it had to do with religion, but I always felt silly pledging allegiance to a flag. How could someone tell me this is what I had to do when no one would ever explain why? Wasn't this the land of the free? Where was the freedom to think for ourselves? I had a problem with my mother's religions too. They all claimed to be the true religion, and if you broke their rules you were going to hell. I wasn't sure I believed in hell, because often I felt like I was living in one.

During the winter, the church brought us jackets and food. My mother depended on the government for assistance, which I know she dreaded. I look back and wonder how my mother ever made it through these trying times. She once cried at a grocery store when a rude cashier rushed her as she fumbled for her food stamps. My sister and I cried too. How did we get here? Everything was beginning to look so bright in Washington, and now we were back where we started, only worse.

My mother was devastated after my father left her. She had been with him for more than nineteen years, and she thought he would never leave. When you fall in love and get married, you naturally believe it's forever. She quit eating and lost a lot of weight. At night, I could hear her cry. It hurt me to watch her. I almost wished he hadn't left. He was an abusive, violent alcoholic, but he was all any of us knew. They fought in court for years. He refused to let her have anything, including the Washington house, but she eventually won.

Through all of her heartache, she chose to fight. She returned to school to further her third-grade education. She learned English, and eventually landed a job working at bankruptcy court during the day and attended school at night. My siblings and I took care of ourselves. My sister went on to make her own friends and suddenly I felt incredibly alone. I had no one. Everything in my life was gone. I couldn't let go of the past and kept in contact by mail and phone with my friends in Washington. One summer, I took a train back to Washington for a visit. As the train reached the little town of Carrolls, I saw the river I loved so dearly. Tears ran down my face as I recalled the day we left. An old man sitting next to me couldn't help but ask if I was leaving my home.

I looked at him and smiled with tears streaming down my face and said, "No, I'm coming home. I'm finally home." I never wanted to leave, but in my heart, I knew things would never be the same.

I learned that I ached for a time in my life, and not necessarily the place. The '70s were gone and we'd moved into a new era. When I returned to Idaho, I fell into a deep depression. My world became dark and lonely. I spent my days in my bedroom, reminiscing about the past. I found the local school druggie and I latched on to him. He was a short guy with a big head, as if all of his drug use had stunted his growth. We were both thirteen years old at the time. He managed to get me stoned every day after school.

One afternoon after school, the short guy with the weed and I got stoned inside the barn behind my house. I smoked and smoked trying to get higher and higher. I wanted to die. Boise never accepted me, and I wanted out. As I sat in the barn, my heart began pounding louder and faster. I thought it was going to burst. The barn exploded into flames and Satan appeared in front of me. Suddenly, everything went black. There was no sound, no sight, no nothing. I entered a cloud and began to walk through it. There was a light and at the end, my sister was standing there, reaching out her hand. She reached for my hand and hugged me.

I leaned forward and whispered, "I'm scared."

She said, "You're fine, Mia. Don't worry. You'll be okay."

In an instant, I found myself running in the Olympics and carrying a torch. In front of me, I saw God with his hands folded. He looked down at me with sympathetic eyes. I said, "God, please forgive me. Get me through this and I swear I'll never get high again." I made a deal with God and he saved me. When I woke up the next day, I was so relieved to be back to normal.

Two days later, I forgot the deal I made with God because I got high again.

We were once again behind my house in a shed and getting high. Once again, I entered a cloud and my hands separated from my body. The devil reappeared. He sat on one shoulder and God sat on the other. I ignored both of them, counting the minutes until this bad trip was over. But it wouldn't stop. Hours passed and I was still in a dreamlike state. I went to sleep and woke up the same way. I collapsed in front of my mother and she rushed me to the hospital where they told her I had overdosed. The local police inspected my weed and they discovered it had been laced. My connection had been lacing my pot all along.

My mother sent me to a therapist who said I was a drug addict. For some reason, those words affected me and something changed inside. When I returned to school, no one spoke to me. My sister reported my hookup, and I was labeled a narc. No one wanted to be seen talking to me. But it was okay, my smoking days were over. I decided to get clean and change my life. I attended Alcoholics Anonymous and went to church. By the time I entered my ninth grade year, I was baptized as a Mormon. They gave me so much support and comfort. I was now on the right path.

CHAPTER THREE

I RETURNED TO TAE KWAN DO AND I PUT MY HEART COMPLETELY INTO IT. A local church held classes so that I didn't have to pay. I played the violin and joined the basketball team. It was the first time I felt like a child. My mother didn't complain, either, because she thought it was keeping me out of trouble. Despite my former reputation, I found a friend who was still willing to talk to me and life seemed a little bit better.

In Idaho, the Division of Motor Vehicles issued licenses at age fourteen, and Washington was only a six-hour drive away. I got back together with my first love and developed a long-distance relationship filled with love letters and the occasional visit to the state that I loved so much. My ninth-grade year was filled with school and activities and I was feeling good until I heard my father was doing better in Orange County, California, where he lived with his new wife and drove a gold Corvette. While we were on welfare, he was living the high life. This made me angry.

In 1982, I entered the tenth grade at Capital High School. I was invited to a party and decided I had been doing so well with my sobriety that I could celebrate with a drink. As I took that first sip, I basked in the warmth that came with every bubble that traveled down my throat. I got a little buzzed and it felt good. I decided that was enough and went home. I was in control, I thought. I continued that pattern for a few more nights until one night I couldn't—or wouldn't, I'm not sure—stop. I got so drunk I woke up on my front doorstep outside our house. My mother was so tired from trying to maintain a household that she never woke to hear me manage to crawl into my bed.

Day after day, it was the same scenario. I would get drunk and wake up somewhere new, maybe a taxicab, a hotel room, the middle of the road, my garage, the backyard, the front lawn, everywhere. My grades swiftly fell, and I began to rebel. I shaved the sides of my head and wore fishhooks for earrings. My school uniform became miniskirts, pumps, and fishnet stockings. New wave was the thing. I consumed A Flock of Seagulls, Duran

Duran, and Yaz. I became aloof and friendless. The one friend I had abandoned me. I think I became too weird, even for her.

I rarely started fights, but I did fight back. My sister and I attended a high school football game when one of my classmates started taunting me with the usual slurs, throwing food and gum into my hair.

My sister grabbed my arm and said, "Let's get out of here." We left and the girl followed us out to the parking lot, continuing to call me out by name. I'd had enough. I turned around and said, "If you don't shut the fuck up, I'll beat the shit out of you!"

She laughed and twirled her long, blonde hair. I took one step back, lifted my right hand, and belted her with a straight into her nose. It busted in the middle and blood sprayed everywhere.

During the commotion, someone called the cops. When they arrived and figured out what happened, they sided with me. The case went to court and I was relieved when the judge announced I was provoked and acted in self-defense. But I didn't win all of my fights. One time, a girl beat me up and my mother was furious. She wasn't mad because I got into a fight, she was furious because I didn't win.

High school was torture. No one looked at me. I was invisible. It was like I didn't exist. It felt like I was scream-ing inside of myself, but no one could hear me. Girls didn't want to be my friend and boys didn't want to date me. I was never asked to prom or any of the high school dances. People mistook my shyness for cockiness, and my bad attitude frightened people.

I didn't want to get close to anyone because I didn't want to get hurt, but no one ever tried to get close to me, so I was often hurt. It wasn't unusual for me to show up drunk for school. By my junior year, I was drinking before, during and after school. Most of the time, I drank by myself, but occasionally I would find another alcoholic.

It's weird to describe anyone that I hung out with as a friend. A friend is someone you share your darkest secrets or wildest dreams with, someone who supports you in good and bad moments, a person who lifts you up to be the best version of yourself. I didn't have any friends. I had acquaintances at most.

There was one girl, an acquaintance, who introduced me to a guy she knew. One day after school, we were messing around in his bedroom. It started to escalate and I wanted him to stop. I asked him to stop but he wouldn't. I begged him to stop and he wouldn't. I screamed for him to stop but he still wouldn't. I was a virgin until that moment when he violently took it away from me.

As soon as I could escape his room, I ran home and buried my ripped clothing inside my closet. I felt disgusted and used. I couldn't stop the images from playing in my mind like a horror movie. I needed them to stop. I thought of ways of killing myself.

One day, my sister found me crying inside my room. I showed her my torn clothing that I had been hiding. I didn't know what happened and I didn't know there was a name for it. My sister told me I had been raped. She wanted to kill him, but I begged her not to say a word. When he called the house, she refused to tell me so that I wouldn't talk to him. The incredibly sick thing about all of this is that I wanted to talk to him.

Abuse was something I was used to. I hated him but I also wanted him. I must have done something to deserve this. It must have been my fault. I didn't know how to handle what I was feeling, so I covered the pain with alcohol.

By my senior year, I was struggling to pass high school. I was determined to leave when I turned eighteen years old. I had given up on capturing the magic that I once knew in Washington and decided to embark on a new adventure in California, my original home. My goal was to survive my grueling last days when I met Curt at a party. He was blonde, blue-eyed, and a popular wrestling star who graduated a year before me. I'd heard of him, but the thought of dating someone so popular never crossed my mind. Everyone in our small town raised their eyebrows when they saw us together. It was my way of thumbing my nose at all of them. I sometimes wonder if it was also his way of thumbing his nose at his controlling and conservative family. He was nice to me and we got along very well, but we drank whenever possible.

In 1985, by the end of the school year, the teachers were tired of me and passed me. Idaho was happy to get rid of me. When I graduated from high school, no one came. It didn't seem important. As I watched my classmates and people I once called friends prepare to celebrate a milestone in our lives, I counted down the days until I could leave Boise.

On graduation night, I went to a party and woke up naked in a hotel room. I didn't know where Curt was. I didn't know where I was or how I got there, which wasn't uncommon. I swore I'd quit drinking and I continued to make deals with God. This time I really meant it, I'd tell myself. But the next day, it was more of the same. It was an endless cycle of drinking followed with remorse followed with more drinking and more remorse.

As drinking became a part of my life, I grew more brazen and didn't care who knew. My sister began to worry when I yelled at her in the parking lot of a Circle K for not moving faster to give me a bottle of TJ Swan, the cheapest bottle of wine at the time. My hands were shaking, my forehead sweating.

I screamed at the top of my lungs, "Give me my fucking bottle!"

She sat motionless with her mouth agape. Something was terribly wrong and we both knew it. I had tears in my eyes as she handed me the bottle. I had to have it. I wasn't trying to get drunk, but I was trying to feel normal.

Somewhere in this vicious cycle, you stop getting wasted and you drink to get rid of the shakes, just to survive and forget about the high that was gone a long time ago. You look for it everywhere and you continue to chase that high you once had in the beginning. You never realize it's gone, but it's over and it will never come back. It's like a relationship that's euphoric in the beginning and loses its luster over time. You keep trying to get back what you once had, but you can't because the relationship has changed. Nothing stays the same. Change—the hardest word in my vocabulary. An alcoholic cannot deal with change. We keep repeating the same mistakes over and over, expecting different results.

My sister told me that I'm like a kid who keeps sticking their hand in the fire and getting burned. Maybe next time it won't hurt as much. I'm compulsive and extremely obsessive, which is probably why I've had success in my career, but it's also maddening to be obsessed with something when the rest of your life is a whirlwind of chaos. It would feel like a lifetime before I finally learned.

In one of the last days before I left Boise, I pulled a knife on my mother. She had a habit of hitting me with whatever object was closest to her. For some reason that never made sense, she started to hit me. For the first time, I realized I was bigger than she and capable of hurting her. I reached into a kitchen drawer and pulled out a knife. I raised it to her throat and said, "If you ever touch me again, I will kill you." It was the last time she ever hit me. Looking back, I don't blame my mother. She had problems of her own and she was trying to control three rebellious teenagers. To this day, I feel her pain. I'm surprised she did as well as she did.

She sometimes had to be a referee whenever my sister and I fought. None of us knew how to resolve conflict. Violence was a part of our household and it's all we ever knew. Weeks later, I stuffed $500 into my pocket and packed my little red Toyota pickup truck and headed to Los Angeles. My mother and my boyfriend stood in the driveway and waved goodbye. I never looked back.

My sister had moved in with my father and was living with him and his new wife in Stockton, California. I didn't have a relationship with my father, but I needed to get some rest, so I decided to spend the night with her. I had driven fourteen hours to get there. I had a long talk with my sister that night, and I confided to her that I was scared, alone, and barely had any money. She looked at me and said, "No guts. No glory." I held onto that moment and those words for a long time. I left the following morning. I knew I was destined for something great, but I just didn't know what. I followed my map to Los Angeles and lived out of my truck for a few days.

I remembered a friend of my sister who moved to Orange County and looked him up. He said I could stay with his girlfriend and their baby for a week. It was a hectic household, but it gave me the rest I needed before jumping into the next chapter of my life. I decided to move to Van Nuys, California. There was no reason except they had me close my eyes and play pin the tail on the city. My thumbtack landed on Van Nuys. So off I went in my little, red pickup truck.

It took a few days to find a place because I only had $500, which was not enough for a down payment on an apartment, including a deposit and last month's rent. I found a Chevron gas station where I could "shower" and clean myself up each day. I had a camper on my truck, so I was able to sleep in it when needed. I finally found a place near Victory and Van Nuys Blvd. in the heart of Van Nuys. It wasn't the best place to live but it was the cheapest. I heard gunshots at night, and drug dealers and prostitutes were always close by. I was able to find a studio apartment with bright orange carpeting and a big oil stain in the middle. I was able to get the rent reduced from $400 to $350. I think the landlady felt sorry for me. On my first night inside my own apartment, there was no one to yell at me or tell me what to do. I was excited and also very alone. But I was finally free from my world of dysfunction.

Even though I was lonely, scared, and broke in Van Nuys, I knew I was better off. I remember calling my dad from a pay phone, hoping he could help me out with some money. He said, "I don't have any money, but you can always go home."

I hung up the phone and knew I'd rather die in Los Angeles than ever go back. It was the reminder I needed that I couldn't depend on anyone but myself. I walked back to my apartment and drowned my loneliness in a bottle. After a few unsettling phone calls with my sister, she grew concerned, packed her bags, and moved to Van Nuys to be with me. I found a job at Strouds Linens making $4.20 an hour. My sister found a job at a retirement home.

Before I left Boise, I promised my mother that I would go to college. I enrolled at LAVC, a local college in Van Nuys, in order to keep my promise to my mother.

Nowadays, college students enroll online with the click of a mouse, but there was a time when students physically stood in line on campus to register for classes. It was there that I was introduced to pills. I met a local dealer while standing in line and we instantly became friends. Leave it to me, in a room full of people, to locate and befriend the dysfunctional one.

We had one thing in common, we loved to be high. He introduced me to uppers and downers. I fell hard for the downers. I always became addicted to depressants and never stimulants. I had so much anxiety that I must have been self-medicating myself. The downers took the edge off and made me feel like I was floating on a cloud with nothing to fear and nothing to worry about.

My dealer wanted more from me than just my friendship, but I wouldn't give him anything else. Yet I desperately needed him because he had something I wanted. His name was Adam. He was unattractive and always wore clothes that were too big for his short and skinny frame. His hair was dark and his eyes were vacant—you could tell he was bad. I made sure I was nice to him. I often teased him, leaving him with the hope that one day we would be a couple. In exchange for the possibility, he kept supplying me with pills. Adam was deceptive, and he would lie, cheat, and steal any chance he could. It sickened me to pretend I was his friend. I hated myself for being a phony.

My sister and I struggled to make ends meet, and I needed more money to support my drinking habit. We added a few roommates to our studio apartment where everyone slept on the floor. While browsing through the newspaper, I saw the answer to my prayers. It was advertisement that read: Club Starlight, Make $600 a night! I immediately phoned the club. It was located at 2nd Street and Broadway in downtown Los Angeles. Men paid a $20 cover, walked into the club, and chose a girl to share drinks, or dance, or play pool. The goal was to keep the guy entertained for as long as possible because not only would you make tips, but you were paid for each minute he stayed.

Each night the girls sat in a group inside the lobby waiting for a man to enter and, hopefully, to be the one he'd pick. If you were selected, the woman in charge would motion for you to sit next to the customer. Sometimes the men were looking for a friendly conversation, and then there were some who wanted to dance. It was completely harmless. We smiled and pretended to be absolutely fascinated with these men. The phoniness began to wear on me. The men were usually middle-aged, wealthy, and horny. They were repulsive but the money was decent. Between customers, I would get completely wasted. My regular customers usually brought me alcohol to the non-alcoholic facility.

Leaving the club, I began noticing some of the girls with nice cars, clothes, and jewelry. I began to wonder how they made so much money. One evening, one of my regulars came in and tipped me $200. I was thrilled! The next time he came in, he tipped me $2,000! I couldn't help but brag to the rest of the girls.

One of the girls asked, "What did you do for it?"

I was shocked and angry. "Nothing!" I said indignantly.

She looked at me and said, "Not yet, but you will."

I couldn't believe she thought I'd done something, or that I ever would. I would never prostitute myself. But that's how it starts, and they all knew it but me. First, the men get you addicted to the money. Then when they think they have you hooked on cash, they spring it on you. "Mia, you know, I've been coming here for a while and paying you good money, and I've never asked for anything in return. I don't think I can keep this up anymore." They watch you freak out as you think about all the bills you have to pay. Then it happens again. "Mia, if you do something for me, I'll do something for you." They wait patiently for you to break down because they know you will. It's just a matter of time. I was disgusted and walked out. One month later, I went back. The bills needed to be paid, tuition was due, and I had a habit to pay for.

At first, he just wanted to touch my breast on the outside of my blouse. He told me that touching my breast was great, but if I wanted his help, it wouldn't be enough. "Forget it!"

He waited patiently.

"What do you want?"

He wanted a hand job.

All I could think about were my bills, tuition, my habit. It made me sick. I cried in the bathroom, wondering how I ever got here. I broke down, and as expected, it eventually wasn't enough.

Another month later, he told me, "If you don't give it up, I will never help you again."

I broke down once again. I laid in the bed stiff as a board and cried the entire time. He paid me ten grand to sleep with him. He threw money on the bed and walked out. I drowned my pity in a bottle of tequila along with a few Valiums. It wasn't enough to make the memory disappear. No matter how hard I scrubbed in the shower, I couldn't wipe it away. I stared at the ceiling and my eyes were blank, just like my sister's when my dad beat her soul out of her body. My mind went blank and removed itself from my body. When you're in that much pain, your soul tries to save itself. I must not crumble. I must not be defeated. I never went back to the club. I tried to erase it from my life, but in my heart I always knew it was there.

I used the money for my sister and I to upgrade to a one-bedroom apartment in North Hollywood. I eventually dropped out of school because it was interfering with my drinking. I found a job at a tanning salon where I met a bodybuilder named Lonnie. He had tattoos all over his body. He had light brown hair, green eyes, and a beautiful tan. He rode a motorcycle, and he was definitely a bad boy. Two dysfunctional people met and fell for each other, but Lonnie didn't drink. He was a recovering alcoholic and had been sober for two years. When my sister moved back to Idaho, I moved in with Lonnie. I wanted to make a clean start.

I vowed to give up drinking and using. I wish I could say my relationship with Lonnie was a good one, but it wasn't. On our first date, he told me he didn't like Mexicans because they were lazy, and they smelled. I should've gotten up and walked out the door, but I stayed. I just couldn't see him for what he was—a racist piece of trash. It only got worse from there. Lonnie had a mean streak in him. He would come home from a bad day at work and beat on me to release tension. I was often left with black eyes and bloody lips. One time, he tied me to a pole and made me take off my clothes so he could beat on me without me moving. It was easier for him. I dealt with his abuse by drowning myself in booze. Lonnie was very jealous and watched me like a hawk. I gave up my job at the tanning salon. I couldn't function anymore.

One day when he was at work, I rummaged through his things and found different forms of identification from different states. As I searched through stacks of paper and documents, I discovered he was wanted in several states. In one state, he was imprisoned for nearly beating his girlfriend to death. When he came home, I threatened to leave him. He beat me so badly that the neighbors called the police. I defended him and took the blame. He left me that night.

Believe it or not, I was devastated and begged him to stay. Deep down, I knew God was doing for me what I couldn't do for myself. I got completely inebriated and drove my pickup into a telephone booth. I staggered to the phone and called my father. I have no idea why. I guess I was hoping he would act like a father and come to my rescue. I needed a father, but like my entire life, he was nowhere to be found. I drank until the sun came up. I wanted to give up. I'd had it with this life and I couldn't go on living this way. Once again, I wanted to die. I felt if I had to go one more day drinking and using, I would just rather die because this was death. Someone kill me and end this suffering. I was in a dark tunnel that I couldn't escape and there was no light at the end to guide me. I felt hopeless. I saw myself running and longing to emerge into the light but there wasn't any. I sat inside my truck longing to die. I suddenly remembered Lonnie once took me to an Alcoholics Anonymous meeting somewhere on Whitsett Avenue. I couldn't remember exactly where it was, but I started driving toward it. As I drove along, I saw a crowd standing outside a house. That had to be it, I thought. I pulled over and walked up to the house, where people greeted me with welcomes.

By the grace of God, I found the place. God was directing me toward the light. He answered my prayers and at that moment I knew it wasn't my time to die. God had something planned for me. I just didn't know what.

I sat alone in the back and listened to people pour their hearts out about their battles with alcohol and drugs. I found myself nodding along and agreeing with everything I heard. I listened to them talk about their vows to quit drinking and their promises to God, but always falling short. I heard their stories about their lack of self-esteem and their desire to be loved. Many more talked about how they never felt comfortable in their own skin and never felt a part of anything meaningful. I found solace in knowing I wasn't alone. There were people just like me and for the first time in my twenty years of life, I felt like I belonged.

At the end of the meeting, a man named Jimmy came up to me and asked if I was coming back the next day. I said I didn't know, but I was flattered and relieved that someone acknowledged me. I wasn't invisible. Someone saw me. Someone wanted me to come back.

I came back the next day and then the next and then the next. I never left. One day, I raised my hand and said, "Hi, I'm Mia, and I'm an alcoholic."

I felt as though an elephant was lifted off my chest. For the first time, I finally emerged from the darkness. It was a new day and a new life. I often look back and wonder if I died that day in the barn. Did God save me? Sometimes, I wonder how many times I've died in my life.

My dad once told me if I pretended to be someone long enough, I would become that person. I wanted to be the young girl in Washington, but no matter how hard I willed it to happen, I couldn't get back there. In my dreams at night, I went back. I'd see myself running up the gravel hill to my house with my dog running alongside me. I ran so fast, but yet, I could never get to my home. I ran in circles and couldn't find it. My dream slowly becomes a nightmare. I'm running through time and I can't go back. I drop to my knees and grab my stomach because the pain is unbearable. My sister appears and tells me, "You're searching for a time in your life and not a place. You can't find it because it's gone. It doesn't exist anymore."

When I wake up, I'm devastated. I think back to when I was eighteen and my drug counselor told me I could always go back, but only when I fell asleep at night. He said it's in my mind and it's always there, it's just not in my conscious world. He told me it will always be there waiting for me whenever I need it.

CHAPTER FOUR

ONCE AGAIN, I RETURNED TO TAE KWAN DO WHERE I WORKED TOWARD EARNING MY BLACK BELT. I enrolled in community college and I got a job working with at-risk youth who battled drug addiction. During this time, I managed to book a few modeling and acting jobs so I could pay the bills. But most importantly, I made time to attend AA meetings.

My mother's voice was always in my head. Even when she wasn't around, I could always hear her telling me that knowledge is power. She demanded that I get an education. Little did I know then that my education would empower me in ways that I never imagined. My mother shared Buddha's philosophy—whatever you put into the world, you'll get back. If you want something, you will it to happen. I had a lot of goals, but I needed to start with getting sober.

I had one slip where I had to give my drug use one more try. It didn't work out and on August 7, 1988, I started over. This time, I had to completely turn my life over to a higher power and come to the realization that I couldn't do it on my own. I was powerless and only something bigger than myself could restore my sanity. I recommitted to AA and that's where I met the love of my life.

It was called the Musician's Meeting because a lot of musicians, and some actors, attended this particular meeting. During a break, everyone would go outside to smoke a cigarette in the parking lot and that's when I noticed Kristoff St. John. He was checking me out. He was beautiful.

He had mocha brown skin and big, brown eyes. His lips were full and his face was chiseled like a model. He was 6'2" inches tall, lean, and strong. I turned to my friend and said, "Oh my God. He's in that show!"

Kristoff was an actor who appeared in the CBS prime time show *Charlie & Co.*, and he played the son of Flip Wilson and Gladys Knight. I remembered him well because I watched the show every week with my sister, who had the biggest crush on him. To annoy her, I would talk about how stuck up he looked and tell her how he wasn't all that. My sister would just roll her eyes. But on this day, I thought of what my sister once said, "No guts. No glory."

During our next break, I decided to go for it. He was talking to an acquaintance of mine who called me over and introduced us. I was wearing black tights and cowboy boots with an oversized black-and-white shirt—it was the ultimate '80s uniform. He was wearing a T-shirt and ripped jeans. I pretended not to know who he was and asked him, "What do you do?"

He told me he was an actor. He was funny, vibrant, and very charismatic. At one point, while we chatted, I looked up at him and our eyes met. I felt my heart leap out of my chest. I smiled and looked down at my feet, something I did whenever I blushed. The blood rushed to my face and I turned beet red. I couldn't make it stop.

As soon as I got home, I called my sister and told her, "I just met the man I'm going to marry and I'm going to have his children."

It was more than hope. It was destiny.

After our first meeting, we were inseparable. We spent every moment we could together, and when we were apart, he consumed every thought. I'd never felt like this before. I'd only seen it in the movies and I never, not for one moment, thought someone could actually be swept off their feet. But there I was, completely lovestruck. We attended a lot of meetings together. When I met him, Kristoff had been sober for a few months after completing rehab at St. Joseph's Hospital.

One night, we were supposed to meet at AA, when he didn't show up. As soon as it ended, I marched out of the meeting and I was fuming because I thought he had stood me up. As soon as I got to the parking lot, he was sitting inside his ivory-colored Jeep that he loved so much. He had a guitar in his hand, and he was waiting for me. He began to serenade me right there in front of the whole world. He sang John Denver's "Sunshine On My Shoulders" and I melted. As he sang, tears rolled down my cheeks because I knew no matter what happened in our lives, I would love this man until the end of time.

Neither of our parents approved of our relationship. I was twenty-one years old and Kristoff was twenty-two. His parents didn't approve of any relationships because they assumed every woman he met only wanted his money. My mother did not support our mixed-race relationship. Kristoff and I didn't care what our parents thought, and we swiftly moved into an apartment in Studio City, California. *Charlie & Co.* was cancelled after a single season, but he quickly found a job on *Generations*, a soap opera that launched in March 1989. Shortly before he started, we found ourselves talking about our future while at a restaurant.

Kristoff looked at me and said, "Let's have a baby." I smiled and said, "Okay."

We were young, in love and it seemed like the most natural conversation to have. The following month, I found out I was pregnant. We had no idea what we were in for. While he worked, I continued going to school and working at a boys' home, which benefitted my degree. Kristoff made enough money that I didn't have to work, but I was not the type to stay at home.

At a young age, I learned to never rely on a man. I always intended to be my own person and make my own money. I resented it whenever a boyfriend tried to tell me what to do. I was bullheaded and stubborn. Kristoff always said I wanted to wear the pants in the family. At times he found it endearing, but it was also the root of many fights. He was used to always getting his way. He had been an actor since he was seven years old, when he appeared in *Roots: The Next Generations*. Adults were catering to him his entire life, until I came along.

There were days when we couldn't keep our hands off each other, but then there were moments when we wanted to kill each other. We were blinded by our emotions and didn't realize the few things we had in common—we were young, controlling, and addicts.

On December 3, 1989, one week before the birth of our son, Kristoff didn't come home. He went to work in the morning but hadn't returned. I quickly grew concerned and I phoned his family and friends, but no one knew where he was. We all feared the same thing.

His parents, Maria and Christopher, were familiar with his disappearing acts and didn't share my fear that something had happened to him. I was convinced he was in a horrible car accident with no way to call for help, or maybe he was violently mugged while walking to his car, or maybe he was taken against his will and tied up in an abandoned warehouse. My hormones were surging, and I couldn't help but think of the worst possible scenarios.

I never thought it was his choice. What do you mean he's using? No way! We're sober, we have a baby on the way, it's not possible. I didn't sleep that night. I called hospitals and jails across the Los Angeles area. I couldn't stay at home and wait, so I drove around the city and searched frantically for him. Tears ran down my face as I called out his name. It was late and I drove around aimlessly. The city was too big and I didn't know where to start. I reluctantly went home, where I paced for hours waiting for each minute to pass. It was 2 a.m., then 3, then 4. I finally watched the sunrise. The first thing they teach us in Alcoholics Anonymous is to take care of ourselves, but I couldn't eat or sleep. I knew I had to; I was due to give birth in a couple of days. Around 7:30 a.m., the phone finally rang. I was both relieved and terrified. It was his grandfather calling to tell me they found Kristoff.

I had a million questions. "Where is he? How is he? What happened?"

His grandfather wouldn't give me details, but said he was in no shape to be seen. I eventually learned Kristoff has been up all night and smoking crack. I couldn't believe it, or maybe I didn't want to. When he finally came home, his mouth was black from the pipe smoke and his eyes were red and distant. He was as far away from me as he could be. He cried as I held him. I didn't know it then, but I was co-dependent, and I nursed him back to health. I cleaned him, made him something to eat and put him to bed. Throughout all of it, I kept asking myself "Why?" What in his life could be so bad that he had to turn to the darkness with such an evil drug? What did I do? How can I fix it? In my heart, I knew I couldn't fix him but I had to try.

I was lost in my confusion when pain shot through my stomach. It tightened and continued to increase by the hour. At 3 a.m., I grabbed Kristoff's shoulder and told him I was in labor. He was probably still half-loaded, but he rushed me to the hospital. Two hours later, it was time for him to go to work. My mother-in-law stayed with me and held my hand while we waited for my baby, but also quietly thinking about Kristoff. When I was ten centimeters dilated, the show let Kristoff come be by my side.

At 5:45 p.m. on December 5 in Tarzana, California, Julian St. John was born. He was 8 lbs. and 9 oz. We cried as we held our first little angel in our arms. At that moment, he became the most important thing in my life.

I was determined to stay sober and give him the best life possible. Kristoff was determined as well—at least, he convinced me of it.

I never questioned Kristoff's love for Julian. Kristoff loved him dearly and was a doting father. There was never any question of it. It was his love for himself that left me unsure. I never used crack or cocaine or anything like it, so I can't fathom how fiercely this drug grabs ahold of its user and takes him down. Every addict eventually hits bottom, but crack takes you down with the weight of an anvil tied around your neck. Every addict has their drug of choice, and crack was his.

On December 25, Kristoff got down on one knee and gave me the most beautiful diamond ring I had ever seen. He sang Joe Cocker's song, "You Are So Beautiful To Me." I cried and jumped at the chance to say yes. He was a romantic at heart, and when he opened himself up and gave me everything I wanted, there was nothing I wouldn't do for him.

Shortly afterward, *Generations* was cancelled, but Kristoff was picked up by the soap opera *The Young and the Restless*, where he would go on to portray fan-favorite Neil Winters. The money was better, and the show was ranked number one. For the next few months, we lived in bliss—we adored our new baby, we celebrated our engagement, and he was an instant hit on his new show.

I still attended school, where I often strolled Julian into class. Many times, I nursed him. I nursed him everywhere—our Sunday bowling league, inside restaurants, wherever it needed to be done. I was a New Age mom and believed it was natural. I didn't believe in weaning, so I breastfed him until he was three years old. However, I don't recommend it now. When your child can run up to you and tell you he wants to be breastfed, it's time to wean.

I quit attending Tae Kwon Do until I could find a new coach. I was devoted to raising my son and continuing my education. If Julian couldn't go to school with me, he spent the day at the soap opera set with his father and a part-time nanny. I finally left community college and transferred to California State University at Northridge, where I majored in psychology. I had always been interested in human behavior, but more importantly, I wanted to know why I was the way I was.

Despite having a difficult time in high school, I loved going to school. I loved learning and I loved to read. I found it challenging and I always felt productive. I realized the more I learned, the more questions I had. I would drown in my thoughts as I asked myself existential questions: Why are we here? What is my purpose? Where do we go after we die? I searched for the answers even though I'm still trying to answer these same questions many years later.

Before I had Julian, I'd get in my red truck and drive fifteen hours to visit my mother in Boise. At night, I'd be the only person on the highway, and I'd stare at the countless stars that extended to the horizon. Even though there was no one around, I'd ask myself a hundred more questions along the way.

Kristoff tried his best to support me, but I think he felt threatened as I continued to grow. At school, I took advanced psychology classes to meet my requirements, but I enrolled in an art history class for me. I fell in love with the Impressionists, from Gauguin to Renoir to Van Gogh. I bought dozens of books about the Impressionists and read about them every free moment I had. Kristoff didn't understand. I think he wanted a wife who spent her days cooking and cleaning and making a perfect home for her husband. I did the best I could, but I was too much of a free spirit to spend my life constrained at home. I wanted my own life. We were butting heads and our fights grew more frequent and increasingly toxic. There was not enough room for the three of us inside our home.

Kristoff left shortly after Julian's first birthday. He went on a drinking binge and celebrated his single life. I refused to ask about him because I didn't want to know who he was celebrating with or where. Two months later, Kristoff came back. He told me he was scared of everything moving so quickly in his life. He wasn't prepared for the responsibility that came with being a parent, and perhaps neither was I. When he moved back in, I got pregnant with our daughter Paris.

When I was four months pregnant, we finally got married. I think he felt it was his obligation to walk me down the aisle. The night before our wedding day, his father and cousin kidnapped him. My family and I sat up all night wondering if there would even be a wedding. Waiting up all night for Kristoff to come home had grown tiresome, but now I was furious. He finally escaped from his family at 4 a.m. I was so angry that I knew we'd get divorced. So why did I go through with it? I think it was for my children, and probably a part of me still loved him.

Despite this, Kristoff arranged the most beautiful wedding a girl could ever imagine. The Calabasas Country Club was overflowing with red and white roses as we overlooked the California sunset. Both of our families and the cast from *The Young and the Restless* attended the ceremony. It was magical. Shortly afterward, we brought Julian with us for our honeymoon on an extravagant cruise to the Bahamas.

We managed to forget our problems and celebrate our lives together, but the fairy tale quickly came to an end.

Two weeks after the wedding, Kristoff asked for a divorce.

Like I said, I knew it wouldn't be long. I was eight months pregnant when I grabbed my son and moved out. I held my head high and swore I would never shed another tear for that man as long as I lived. "I won't crumble," I told myself over and over. If my mother could survive after my father left her with three children, without any money or a job, and the inability to speak English, I could certainly survive this. Thankfully, Kristoff always made sure I had the means to raise our children.

I got an apartment not far from him, and once I was fully moved in, I enjoyed being in the comfort of my own place. I realized I didn't particularly like sharing my living space with anyone. It was always a hard adjustment for me. Kristoff and I always remained in each other's orbit. When I went into labor for the second time, Kristoff was, once again, by my side. Regardless of our dysfunctional relationship, I never questioned my decision to have Paris St. John.

My second little angel came to me on April 30. She weighed 7 lbs. 15 oz. My love for her was infinite. The hardest part was for my son. Every day, he waited by the front door for his dad to come home.

I tried explaining to him that his father lived and worked away from us. It was the hardest thing I'd ever had to do. Julian was my heart and I'd rather rip off my right arm to spare him any pain in his life before letting him feel the disappointment of a father never coming home.

Julian was never the same. He became angry and blamed me. He clung to his father like he never had before.

When Paris was born, I felt like I had lost my son. I went through a severe bout of depression. On top of that, I couldn't get out of bed for two weeks because the epidural I'd been given cut through my spine. I couldn't care for myself or my children. The depression felt like a never-ending cycle. I decided to go back to the one thing that brought me solace in my life—competition. When Julian was a baby and I took Tae Kwon Do, it was too relaxed and not competitive. This time, I'd heard of a more competitive gym called All Pro Tae Kwon Do with a coach named Mr. V.

He was strong, stern, and a no-nonsense man. He had very little sympathy for my plight or attitude. He started me out as a red belt, one level below a black belt. He was going to make me prove myself all over again. When I first arrived, there were times when I was tired, or I didn't feel like giving it my all. I was still feeling sorry for myself.

Mr. V kicked me out every time. He told me not to return until I could commit 100 percent. I finally crumbled. He screamed at me in front of the entire class and told me to get out. "Don't come back until you stop feeling sorry for yourself! You're weak! You'll never make it! Stand up and fight!" I'm not sure what specifically resonated with me, but it lit a fire inside of me that had already been kindling.

From that day forward, I came in every day with a purpose. I ran every morning. I started lifting weights. I trained every night. I competed in every tournament I could. Mr. V taught me about passion. He taught me to bring my passion into the ring. I'd attend tournaments and girls would withdraw knowing they had no chance against me. When we did fight, I fought them with the intent of hurting them and I didn't care how I did it.

Afterward, I would feel badly but never during our competitions. My opponents were the perfect victims for all of my rage. Sometimes, I could hear myself screaming inside of me. All of the injustices I endured throughout my childhood, all of my failed relationships, my father's abuse, it all came pouring out of me in the ring.

Mr. V made me get a DBA, or a fictitious name like "The Italian Stallion" from *Rocky*. I asked why. He saw my potential before I did. He said, "You may not need one now but someday you will." I picked the name, "Knockout." At that moment, I hadn't considered the world of boxing.

CHAPTER FIVE

While Kristoff took the children to the soap opera set, I was growing more committed to my career in Tae Kwon Do. In 1996, I told my trainer that I wanted to compete in the 2000 Sydney Olympics. He supported me and told me I would have to train like never before. I was mentally prepared, but now I needed to focus physically. But I was twenty-nine and the girls competing were in their teens. I was at the end of my amateur career and I knew it. As much as I believed in myself, I needed to start making a living. Even though I felt like I could have beaten all of those girls, I had to go bigger. I left Sydney behind and turned to boxing.

My coach was dead set against it. "The injuries are not worth it," he said. "You'll become brain damaged and before you know it, the business will chew you up and spit you out."

He tried to talk me out of it. One of the other coaches overheard me and told me he knew of a trainer who could possibly help me. If there was no way to talk me out of it then he might as well help me.

In September of 1996, I met Art Lovett. He met me at the studio one afternoon. He wasn't like my other coaches. He had a diamond earring in each ear, and he wore a bandana around his head. He told me he was looking for a project of his own—a fighter he could bring up from scratch. The only problem was I was a girl, and none of the local gyms allowed female boxers at the time. We trained at the park.

Art was sweet even though he tried to act rough and mean. He was a teddy bear underneath it all. Don't get me wrong, we butted heads a lot, especially since he wanted me to completely give up Tae Kwan Do. I was torn, but I came to love boxing more. I wasn't very good yet, but boy, did I have heart.

Art used to put me in the ring with top-notch girls and I'd get my butt kicked every time. He said he wanted to see if I'd come back. I came back every time. When I was in the ring, I fought like my life depended on it. My skills were primitive, but you'd have to kill me to put me down. The other girls may have been equipped with their technique, but I made sure I was never the first to quit. I told Art I wanted to sign with Don King Productions, the best promoter at the time. And I wanted to fight Christy Martin, a professional boxer who'd signed with Don King. She had a string of knockouts and was considered the best female boxer. I also wanted to open for Oscar De La Hoya. Some people may have considered them dreams, but they were my goals.

Art looked at me and smiled, he patted me on the back and said, "All in good time." I was serious. I was going to sign with Don King. He just didn't know it yet.

I signed with Dan Goossen, a top promoter, but not as big as the top guys such as Bob Arum and Don King. I turned pro and fought my first professional fight on the undercard of fighter Gabe Ruelas at the Fantasy Springs Casino on February 14, 1997, in Indio, California.

I sat in my dressing room with Art and my mom, who'd become my pseudo manager. Our relationship had gotten better through the years, especially when she acknowledged my dedication to the sport. She never missed a fight and she was, literally, in my corner.

She could tell I was nervous. I wondered how I would possibly climb through the ropes. My legs were shaking and sweat was dripping from everywhere. As Art carefully used tape to wrap my hands, I could tell he was scared too. I was his Little Girl, which he often called me. He protected me, and now he felt helpless. He became more like a father to me rather than a trainer.

I looked up at him and said, "Art, I'm scared."

He said, "So am I. Let's go out the back."

I started to laugh. We all laughed and it was exactly what we needed.

A fighter's fear is the unknown—not knowing what will happen in the ring. Countless questions fill your head. Will I get knocked out in front of everyone? Will I be injured? Will I die? Or will I be victorious? The fear of the unknown left me paralyzed with anxiety.

There was a knock at the door. "You're up in five."

Walking through the tunnel is like walking to the gallows. The crowd is rabid, the lights are blinding, and all eyes are focused on you. Your team walks ahead of you and your face is stoic because the anxiety has left you frozen. You wonder how you'll ever get your arms and legs to move because they feel like rubber. You want to vomit because the butterflies in your stomach have reached your throat. Then the mind games begin. "You won't make it. You're going to choke. You're not ready."

Then it's time to meet at the center of the ring. The ref gives his instructions and you can't hear a word of it. Everything is happening in slow motion. And then the clang of the bell rings through the arena.

Instantly, your instincts kick in. You forget the crowd and everything around you. There's only one thing on your mind. You must win. Instead of worrying about how I would get started, I realized I should have worried how I would stop. I always had trouble stopping when the bell signaled to end the round. The ref usually had to jump in.

I fought Angelica Villain and knocked her out in fifty-four seconds of the first round. Art jumped into the ring and lifted me up on his shoulders. It was the ultimate thrill. Victory was my drug.

That feeling was better than any high I'd ever experienced in my life. I thought I'd never come down, but like with any high, you always do. The crash was depressing and it quickly engulfed me. I would take stimulants like ephedrine before my fights to get me going, so the crash was not just an emotional thing, but a physical thing too. So, what do you do? Like an addict, you fight again. I couldn't stop. I was sparring, running, and lifting every day, anything for the high. It was my entire life.

I sent a letter to Don King despite everyone telling me I could not just go to the top, but I had to work my way up there. No one could give me a sufficient explanation as to why I needed to wait. When I want something, I go after it—and I wanted Don King.

One day, on our way to training, Art received a phone call. His mouth dropped. "Yes, we're interested," he said. "Of course we'll come out."

He hung up and I could hardly handle the suspense. "Who was it," I demanded.

"Don King Productions!" he yelled. "They got your letter, and they want you!"

We sat in Art's car and screamed loudly as tears rolled down our cheeks.

I fought one more fight for Dan Goossen, which resulted in a TKO, a technical knockout that meant my opponent was injured and the referee declared me the winner. Afterward, I left for Florida to sign with Don King Productions.

We flew in first class and prepared for my first national TV interview on the popular entertainment show *Inside Edition*. I was billed as Don King's newest knockout. I signed a three-year deal for more money than Art had ever dreamed I would make.

My professional debut was slated for June 21, 1997. We arrived in Florida one week before the fight so we could do press and stir up energy. Somehow, I knew that fight would put me in the press like no other. Something big was going to happen.

Unfortunately, something big does not always mean something good. On the plane, Art was taking his heart medication more often than usual. After one of our early running sessions, his legs started turning blue and purple. I was concerned that he was still sneaking cigarettes after he'd promised me that he would give up smoking. He kept assuring me he was fine. He was my protector, he reminded me, and I needed to worry about him less and focus on the fight in front of me.

One afternoon, I went for a run and returned later than I expected. When I returned, Art was pacing and waiting for me outside the hotel. When he saw me, he flashed a huge smile filled with relief and stretched out his arms to give me a hug. He was so happy I was okay. He hugged me so tight that I laughed. Secretly, I was happy he cared so much for me. My mother was set to arrive a few days later, so it was nice always having him around.

I had no sparring partners in Florida, so Art made himself available. It was a sweltering, hot day in Florida, and the gym was ten times hotter and more humid than usual. Art was wearing his infamous plastic Santa suit that made him sweat, as we sparred that day. At one point, I bloodied his nose, but he encouraged me to continue.

Reluctantly, I laid a straight right, a power punch, directly into his chest. He stopped in his tracks and as I pulled back, he slid down the ropes to the canvas. I went back to my corner and threw my hands up. I was mad, but it was only because I was scared. I didn't know what was happening. I went back over to him and knelt beside him.

"Damn it, Art! Damn it!" I yelled.

He told me he was okay. "I just need to sleep for a bit," he said as he curled up in a fetal position in the middle of the ring.

All I could do was scream for someone to call 911. There were cameras filming me that day and I demanded for them to be turned off. Art begged me not to let them take him to the hospital.

I raised my voice and said, "If you don't go to the hospital, I'm calling off this fight! I won't fight without you." I cried. I always told him this before every fight.

He'd say, "I know. You can't fight without me."

But this time, he looked up at me and said, "Yes, you will."

He wasn't laughing. He was letting me go. I begged him to go to the hospital and he said, "OK, I'll go if you come with me."

I rode to the hospital with him, and everyone reassured me that he was going to be fine. After we got there, the doctor said Art was just overheated and he'd be okay. I walked outside to sit in the sun while taking a break from the chaos inside the hospital. I had his wallet with me and started looking through it.

He had his license and a couple of credit cards, but he also had photos of him and his family. I realized he had an entire life that I didn't know anything about. I was so selfish with him. We did everything together. We trained, went to the movies, went to eat, and ran errands together, and yet he had a family this entire time. He gave me his whole life. I couldn't imagine one without him.

At that moment, his doctor came outside to tell me Art went into cardiac arrest and they did everything they could to save him. From then on, my memory is a blur. I can remember standing up and running through the hospital while screaming. They ushered me into a room by myself and I fell to the floor, wailing at the top of my lungs. My cries were heard throughout the hospital. I told the doctors I had to see him because my heart wouldn't let me believe he was gone.

I saw him lying there with a tube still down his throat. His body was lifeless, but I told him everything I always wanted to say and never did. I told him how much I loved him and how he was the only father I ever had. I said I was sorry for all of the fights we got into. I thanked him for everything he did for me, for the part of his life that he gave me. I had no idea how I was going to go on.

I looked up and saw Carl King, Don King's son standing at the doorway. I knew the press was going to have a field day with this. I was instructed to tell the press and the police that I was sparring with someone else and not Art. My mom arrived that evening and I fainted in her arms. It was a nightmare, and I was never going to wake up from it. Something big, indeed, happened that week, after all.

After Art was gone, I didn't know how I would continue without him. I only knew then I was afraid that as time went on, he would slip away from me. I wanted time to stand still. I wanted to keep him with me as close as I could. I was afraid that I would forget details about him, like his laugh or the way he held his arms up to hug me. I knew someday it would be a distant memory. I feared this and I didn't want to go to sleep that night. If I could slow down time, I thought, or if I could possibly turn it back, maybe I'd capture one last glimpse of him.

But as I drifted off to sleep in a puddle of tears, he came to me. He was standing on the hill that we used to run together, and he held out his arms to hug me like he always did. He was there, he was really there. It was as real and vivid as if I were awake. And then the inevitable happened, time passed. My heart healed, but there are times when my heart still aches for him. As volatile as our relationship was at times, we had passion for the game and we loved each other.

Pat Goossen began training me after Art died. He was one of the infamous Goossen brothers. They were infamous in the San Fernando Valley. There were ten brothers who started a gym and a promotion company called Ten Goose. The Goossen family grew up in the Valley and posted a strong mark on the boxing world. Some of their kids fought in the game, a couple of them were trainers, one was a promoter, and another was an attorney. Together, they built themselves quite an empire—until the feud began. Two of the brothers tangled over who'd be the leader, so they broke apart and traveled in separate directions. Dan Goossen became one of the biggest promoters in boxing, while his brother Pat remained a trainer. Joe Goossen worked with his older brother Dan as a trainer and their careers flourished. I admire Dan because in the beginning, he wasn't a threat to anyone. Nowadays, he has become, arguably, one of the top three promoters in the world.

Pat began training me at a gym called Jeopardy in Van Nuys. His sons Chuck and PJ, who were also fighters, became my sparring partners. Pat and I began devising a plan to get out of my contract with Don King. We knew we had to get him to believe I was leaving him for Dan Goossen, who at the time, was not a threat. If Don King had an inkling of a thought that I was leaving him to join his rival Bob Arum, he would have never let me go.

Pat did all of his dealings with Arum away from the office. Arum agreed to sign me as long as I had a release from King. Pat dealt with Arum while Mike, his brother and attorney, dealt with King. At first, King wanted to be repaid for the money he claimed he invested in me despite the money he still owed me. King believed I would go nowhere so he released me from my contract in 1998. Less than a month later, I would make my debut for Bob Arum's Top Rank, Inc. on Univision, the number one Spanish network.

The things I've seen on the business side of boxing would make anyone cringe. King was my introduction into the shadier side of boxing, but Arum showed me a darker one. I'm not saying Arum was worse than King, but there was more money and the stakes were shadier. Arum did a lot for my career and was, without a doubt, the smartest promoter in boxing. He could make or break anyone's career. He set out to make me a star and he succeeded. He did for me what Don King did for Christy Martin. Arum planned on exposing me to the world, but first I had to prove myself.

Afterward, I knew what I had to do. I had to find a way to Bob Arum, another top promoter. I fought the rest of my fights with DKP in small-market towns across the United States. I came to realize later in my career that it didn't matter the size of the venue or what network I was on, or who I was fighting, it all felt the same. When I stepped into that ring, my life was on the line.

It didn't matter who was watching, if anyone at all, or if the main event was De La Hoya; it was all the same. The irony of it all is I remember standing in the ring petrified and looking around the arena searching for another human who could possibly feel my pain, my fear, my desperate need to connect with another human being. And there she was, standing in front of me, the only other person that felt my fear and pain, my opponent. Of all the people, only my opponent could relate. And there I was, about to try and rip the life out of her, to demolish her at any expense. It was her or me. But after that day, I always prayed for my opponent, as well as myself, and all the other fighters on the card.

I fought a "trial" fight at the Grand Olympic Auditorium on the undercard for Carlos Palomino in 1998 for a fraction of what King had paid me. I was willing to take the chance. I was determined to be under Arum's promotion.

In the dressing room that night, to my horror, I found out I was going to be announced as Mia Rosales instead of Mia St. John. I was livid and started throwing a tantrum. This was long before the Latin Explosion and there was no one who looked like me. I started to cry. Before that moment, I spent a lifetime downplaying my Mexican heritage in an effort to blend in. My entire life, I had been Mia Richardson and then Mia St. John.

Now, moments before I appeared in front of the world, I was being forced to reveal my true self and I wasn't ready. I was convinced that everyone was going to boo me.

Pat looked at me and said, "Who? The Mexicans? That's all that's out there, honey."

I knew he was right, but I was still unsure. I was afraid of what people would think of me. From the grungy, old dressing room of the Olympic, famous for its fights in the '70s, I made my entrance. This time, I wore hot pink shorts and a sports bra that would become my trademark.

It was the longest walk from my dressing room to the ring, or so it seemed.

As I walked through the tunnel, I could feel the electricity emanating from the crowd. Like sparkling tendrils, I could feel the energy in my fingers and toes. My heart was pounding so loudly, it almost drowned out the crowd. I walked toward the ring and the audience stood on their feet. All I could hear was my heart pounding, and I was unsure what the crowd was going to make of me.

I overheard someone say, "Barbie's going to get her ass kicked."

My opponent was already in the ring. She was extremely muscular and if I didn't know any better, I would have thought she was a man. Her hair was cropped short and she wore *Terminator*-style sunglasses. I don't think she could have been more intimidating. When the announcer yelled my name, "Mia Rosales!" the crowd roared. In an instant, I embraced my heritage and who I was.

Yes, I'm Mexican and they love me.

The Terminator, as she called herself, came out swinging. She was determined to knock Barbie's ass to the canvas, but I was faster, stronger and had more rage in my heart to beat her down. The ref stopped the fight in the second round. The crowd, once again, stood on their feet and roared for their new favorite. It was electrifying. Everyone could feel it, including Arum. He knew he was about to make me a star.

The following week, we signed a deal, but not for the fraction I was paid that night. Instead, I was paid five times the amount King ever paid me, and for three years. I was young and thought those three years would never end. Even when Arum told me it would all be over someday, I didn't believe him. It was a dream come true and I was going to live it to the fullest.

I quickly learned the business.

In the boxing world, The Terminator was what is known as a "tomato can." These fighters are brought in to lose to the promoter's fighter. Now don't get me wrong, these fighters come to fight and win, but their chances are extremely slim.

First of all, the judges are against them, meaning that a fight can usually go either way depending on the scoring. There are no set rules on how to score a fight. A judge could say one fighter had the harder punches, or he had more accuracy, or anything else, just as long as the boss is happy. Honestly, everyone works for the promoter. Even the Commission. Every state has a commissioner who oversees the fights and hires the officials. He is there to protect the fighter and make sure everyone plays by the rules.

Truthfully, his only job is to protect the promoter and make sure the money keeps rolling in. No one truly cares about the fighter. We're just animals in a circus, there to perform on cue, and when they are through with us? We're thrown out to make room for the next favorite, whoever is favored to win, which is usually the one who signed with the promoter.

If he or she loses, it's bad for business. That's the opposite of a tomato can. The quicker you learn this, the better off you'll be. You learn how to have the system work in your favor. Boxing is actually a chess game. It is always about anticipating your opponent's next move, and the promoters', and the commissioners'. In boxing, everyone's always out to outfox someone else. And the promoters have an easier time doing this because they are usually extremely educated and business savvy like Arum.

The fighters, on the other hand, are usually uneducated and trying to work their way out of a ghetto or barrio. It's why so many of them end up broke and broken when it's done. For me, I was educated and had my family's support when it came to business and money. I knew what it meant to be poor, and I was determined never to be poor again.

I feel for the fighters because in this business, it's every man or woman for themselves. No one knows the uncertainty and fear we feel when we walk into that ring, or the pain from the hours of training we do, or the injuries we undoubtedly endure. Tack on the lack of any social and family life, the loneliness, exhaustion from traveling, and never-ending interviews with the media, just to sell a fight. But then again, it's a small collection of people who know the absolute thrill of winning and the adrenaline rush that courses through our entire body when we score a knockout.

Nothing compares to the moment when everyone is cheering and chanting your name. For a brief moment, you're accepted, no matter how shallow, phony, or fleeting it is.

I know that none of it's real because the fans don't really love you and the critics don't really hate you. In the beginning of my career, I would stand and sign autographs for hours and hours. I couldn't get enough attention. The fans meant so much to me. I wanted to please them all.

Eight years later, there came a point when I could hardly wait to get out of the arena and away from the fans. When people would stop me on the street, sometimes I pretended it wasn't me and they must be mistaken. It's not that I don't want to be famous, but after a while you realize that it's fake. The fans don't know the real you, they only love your persona when you're on top. When you're washed up, they'll move on. They always do. You can count on it.

I used to hate going home, where my friends and family treated me like a regular person. No one catered to my every whim, no one there thought I was superhuman. To my kids, I was Mom. To my friends and family, I was Mia. No special treatment. I used to say I could live in the ring forever and never leave the spotlight. But when the hard times came, as they always do, I realized the only people who were truly there for me were my family. They didn't care if I won or lost or how famous I was or how much I made—I always knew they really loved me.

My career lasted more than twenty years, but for three of them, they were glorious. After the Univision fight, I told Pat I wanted to open for Oscar De La Hoya. He laughed and said, "Sure, okay, whatever Mia."

I went to Arum and told him to ask him.

Pat came back later and said, "How would you like to open for De La Hoya versus Chavez on September 19 at Caesars Palace on pay-per-view?"

It was everything I had ever dreamed of. If only Art could see me now!

I arrived in Las Vegas and it was complete madness. The press was everywhere. There were screaming fans outside every facility, and the buzz was heightened from Los Angeles to Las Vegas to Mexico City. I did interviews from 6 a.m. until 1 a.m. the next morning. My mother kept throwing fits and asking how I planned to fight without any sleep. I didn't mind. I was basking in the glory of it all.

Fans waited in the lobby of the hotel, just to get a glimpse of the fighters and hopefully a picture or an autograph. Fans pushed, screamed, and grabbed any limb within reach. Thousands of people would show up just for the weigh-in, mainly to catch Oscar in his briefs and me in my trademark pink bikini.

I met Oscar for the first time at the press conference. It was also the first of many photos that we'd take together. There was gossip that Oscar and I would get together, but it would never happen. I had fun teasing the press, though. Oscar was such a gentleman. He was different than most other fighters. He may not have been formally educated, but he was extremely intelligent. He was business savvy and classy. He was kind, humble, and never said an unkind word about anyone. My mother adored him. We all did. He would go on to fight and defeat Mexico's champion Julio César Chávez. Chavez was a legend in Mexico and being that Oscar was born in America, the crowd was divided. Fight Night contained thousands of loyal fans who would watch the courageous legend throw in the towel after four rounds. But strangely, the crowd remained loyal and never lost any love for Julio Cesar Chavez. He would remain in their hearts forever.

That night, as I took the long walk through the tunnel, the longest walk of a fighter's life, I couldn't see beyond the glaring lights of the arena and the cameras in front of me. The cheers were deafening. I made my entrance for the eighth time in my career. But this time, I was making my debut on pay-per-view on the undercard for Oscar De La Hoya, an achievement for any fighter. Still, I was nervous, shaking, and sweating. It was fight number thirty-five and nothing had changed.

I walked into the ring with Latina superstar Selena's version of "La Bamba." I would use it time and time again. I won a split decision that night and would endure the criticisms of the commentators for many more fights. My wild swinging and aggressive technique did not win the approval of many critics. I took the criticism hard. Learning to box on national television was not easy. Not only did the media attack my skills in the ring, but my personal life, as well.

My next fight was the undercard for De La Hoya versus Quartey, and I flew to New York to promote it. My first interview of the morning was on Howard Stern, an interview that I would live to regret and continues to be replayed.

I've never censored myself. I speak my mind and if people don't like it, it doesn't bother me. Howard probed into my sex life because what I learned is that most people would rather hear about what happens in my bedroom instead of the ring. After much probing into whether I had sexual relations with women, I admitted to being involved with a woman at one time. However, I never said it was a sexual relationship. It ended up in the tabloids, but what made it worse were the made-up stories such as losing custody of my children over it. One story claimed it was the reason Kristoff divorced me. One tabloid said my breast implants ruptured in a fight. The tabloids came out with stories that had absolutely no merit. Of course, the articles also stated that I was a recovering alcoholic, which was true.

After the fight, I received a call from *Playboy* asking me if I had any interest in doing a layout. I told them I'd have to think about it, but after repeated negotiations, I accepted. Part of me was bitter because I was rejected years earlier as a centerfold when I was a teen. Now they wanted me. This time, I would pose as a celebrity, which of course meant a lot more money. Everything works out the way it's supposed to.

Arum and *Playboy* planned for my layout to coincide with the De La Hoya versus Trinidad fight. Don King's girl, Christy Martin, had already landed the cover of *Sports Illustrated*. Arum's girl—me—landed the cover of *Playboy*. The shoot took about a week and was done on location at their studio in Santa Monica. I kept a boxing theme for the pictorial, which included a shower, locker room, and boxing ring. I always wanted the world to remember me for being a fighter.

I once said in an interview for ESPN, "I'm not a *Playboy* model that fights for Top Rank. I am a Top Rank fighter that posed for *Playboy*."

The shoot was harder than any fight. I love fighting. I hate modeling. It's boring. Also, I know it may sound hard to believe, but I'm extremely shy and it was very uncomfortable to be nude in front of a group of cameramen and lighting guys. Originally, I wasn't going to be the cover even though I had asked for it. I kept getting the same response, only Hugh makes that decision.

Shortly after the shoot was complete, I received a phone call. Hugh wanted me for the cover of the November issue, and I needed to come back to shoot the cover photo. I was ecstatic. I was the first boxer to land the cover of *Playboy* magazine and I was making history. Also, I was Mexican, and we all knew Hugh's love of blondes.

I became the lightning rod of women's boxing. The other female boxers despised me. Commentators like Larry Merchant and Teddy Atlas harshly criticized me. Larry was a bitter old man who'd never been in a boxing match his entire life, yet he made his living by cutting down every fighter who ever stepped in the ring. Teddy claimed he fought, but I don't know if he did or didn't. I didn't care. I didn't like him. I bet I could take them both with one arm tied behind my back. I tried to turn the negatives into positives. People were paying attention to me. Whether it was good or bad, my purse continued growing and so did my bank account.

I took limos everywhere, I had my house on a hill, I bought a brand new Mercedes, a jet ski, a car for my mom, property, and investments. My mother warned me against buying a jet ski. She said I shouldn't do any other sports until I was finished boxing. I was so stubborn, I bought it anyway.

One of my first trips out on the jet ski, I wrecked at full speed and ended up in the hospital with a hematoma the size of a grapefruit on my lower leg. I was released from the hospital only to find my leg swollen, black, and blistering four days later. I could only walk with crutches.

I went to Dr. Richard Grossman, a skin specialist at the Grossman Burn Center for whom the center was named. He told me, in the most compassionate voice he could, that I had gangrene and I would need surgery as soon as possible. I burst into tears and refused to accept this. I had a fight in one month and couldn't afford to have surgery now. I asked if it could wait until after the fight. He said the infection could spread to my heart and kill me within twenty-four hours, but he didn't know for sure how long it would take or even if it would happen. I would have to make that decision on my own. He told me to close my eyes and he was going to stick a pin into my leg. He told me to tell him when I felt it. I waited and waited for him to start. He asked me to open my eyes. When I opened them, I saw the pin entirely in my leg. I never felt a thing. I went home, packed my bags, and checked into the hospital for surgery the following morning.

He dug deep to remove all of the dead tissue and took a skin graft from my inner thigh. I spent days in my hospital bed doing sit-ups and using dumbbells to work on my upper body. I escaped my bed every chance I could, and I'd run on my crutches. There was nothing the nurses could do to stop me. I was on a mission.

In the beginning, I was terribly depressed, especially when the doctor told me he didn't know if he could save the muscle in my leg. I stared blankly at the wall for what seemed like an eternity, and then it came to me. No matter what, I would continue to box. Even if it meant boxing one-legged, there was nothing that could stop me. Four weeks later, I was released and began training as hard as I could. My first fight back was on Univision. I fought with a fever but managed to knock out my opponent in the fourth round. I had gone through too much not to win. These were the glory days.

I signed endorsement deals, appeared in guest spots on TV shows playing myself, in commercials, and even appeared in a PlayStation game with EA Sports. It was like a montage straight out of a *Rocky* film. I thought it would never end. After De La Hoya versus Trinidad came De La Hoya versus Coley, De La Hoya versus Mosley, and then my last fight for Top Rank, Roy Jones versus Julio Gonzalez at the Staples Center in Los Angeles. I didn't know it would be my last fight with Arum.

As my career began to explode, Kristoff took over parenting duties. He worked at CBS, so he could just take our two children and the nanny to work with him. I tried taking the children with me when I could, but I was travelling around the world and hotel rooms were no place to raise children. Honestly, the boxing world is a hard enough place for adults, so I was reluctant to bring my children around. I was sober throughout my career. It's easy when winning feels better than using. I admit that I used steroids for most of my career, but it's not unusual in the boxing world. Almost everyone uses steroids. If anyone tells you otherwise, they're lying. I didn't realize until later that my obsession with being a champion was a form of addiction. I wanted to win at all costs. I realize now that I risked my life for the thrill of competition—and a paycheck.

The public doesn't realize the mindset you take in order to be a boxer. In professional boxing, the goal is to render someone unconscious. When I walked into the ring, I was willing to kill another human being. At the same time, I was willing to die for the sport, as well. That's kind of sick when you think about it. Why would anyone do this? You're going to die for a paycheck? You're not even going to be able to spend it! Nothing inside the ring is worth dying for. Die to cure cancer or to fight world hunger, but don't kill another human for sport.

I'll occasionally visit YouTube and look back on videos of my fights. I can't help but admire my body's physique. I was pushing my body to its limits and I was proud of what it could do. But then I have to look away because

I can see the primal look in my eyes. My goal is to destroy anything that comes between me and winning. It's also difficult to watch myself get knocked around. I know that my opponent is trying to kill me at worst, or knock me unconscious at best. But the entire match reminds me of my competitive spirit inside and outside the ring: I get knocked down and I get back up.

CHAPTER SIX

THINGS WERE ALREADY GOING SOUR BETWEEN ME AND ARUM. I had changed trainers numerous times. I was searching for Art and every one of them kept coming up short. I was trying to replace him and finding it hard to accept that no one ever could. I went through several managers, as well. My last manager also worked for Bob Arum. It was considered a conflict of interest. There is a lot of that in boxing. I could tell that Arum was over the pink Playboy Bunny routine, and truthfully, so was I. I wanted to be taken seriously. I wanted to fight tougher fights. I wanted to fight Christy Martin. Arum said she would destroy me. Those words only made me want it more. I had been thinking a lot about my situation and realized I wanted to go out on my own. I didn't need Arum anymore. He had taken me as far as he could—and it was good while it lasted. Somehow, I still wasn't prepared for the end.

That night, I scored a draw against a girl who weighed 11 lbs. more than I did. She was 5 lbs. over the legal limit. The Commission's job was to see that she lost the weight, or she wouldn't fight. Neither happened. It rarely does. To make matters worse, when I received my check at the end of the night, $8,000 was missing. Again, the Commission's job was to see that no deductions were made unless specified before the fight. My money was not returned to me and no one could make Arum do what he didn't want to do, not even the Commission. In fact, Arum told the Commission what to do. He always held the cards.

Afterward, I sat in my dressing room while tears streamed down my face. A variety of emotions swept over me, ranging from anger to fear to sadness. Anger because Arum was killing me by a thousand paper cuts. My career was crumbling one fight at a time until I was washed up. I knew there would come a time when he'd have no use for me. But I didn't want to go out like that. Then the fear of the unknown was setting in. Where will I go? What will I do? I've been to the top. There was no one bigger than Arum. Finally, sadness came over me. I had no choice but to go down the ladder. I wouldn't stay with Arum so I could die a slow death. I'd rather leave with dignity. He still owed me about $70,000 in my contract, but I decided to leave now and try to collect later.

I remember sitting in my dressing room arguing with my mother. She thought I was making a quick and irrational decision. She didn't want me to leave Arum, just like she didn't want to leave King Kong. She wanted me to behave and not make waves. But that's the kind of woman she was—it's how she was raised. I was never like that. After everything she'd seen, how could she still not know me? I did what was right for me. Every time, I followed my heart and never let fear stand in my way. She stood over me yelling, then begging, and finally pleading. I started to drift away in my thoughts. As I looked to the side, I could have sworn I saw Art standing there with our bags packed. He motioned to me with his hand as if to say, "Let's go, Mia. Let's be on our way."

I laughed silently, grabbed my bags, and marched down the tunnel leading out of the arena. I never looked back.

Once I was in the limo, I called Joe Goossen. The Goossens were always there in my time of need. He set me up with a promoter who got me my first fight on ESPN. It wasn't pay-per-view, but it was TV, and the money was pretty good. The fight was to be aired live from San Antonio, Texas, a city that supports boxing and Mexican fighters. It would be my first fight without Arum. I tried to sue Arum for the remainder of my money. The problem was my attorney was also one of Arum's attorneys, and he wouldn't touch the case.

I filed a complaint against the Commission for all their wrongdoings during that last fight with the overweight fighter. I got nowhere on both counts. Instead, all I got were subtle hints to let the matter go, or I would never work again. My attorney urged me to make amends with Arum. My attorney was Sam Perlmutter, best known for the Foreman Grill that made George Foreman, himself, and his partner millions of dollars. I respected his opinion and, reluctantly, I knew he was right.

The following day I sent a letter to Arum thanking him for all that he had done for me and wishing him well. I called the Commission and informed them I was dropping the complaint against them and Arum.

In San Antonio, I fought a southpaw from Georgia who miraculously recovered from hepatitis a few hours after testing positive. In boxing, it is illegal to fight with hepatitis, HIV, or while pregnant, so we are tested for everything before each fight. But it would have cost too much money to bring in a new opponent, and the Commission said she no longer had it. I had never been able to fight a southpaw, a left-handed fighter. Arum never put me in the ring with one. A lot of fighters have a hard time adjusting to them and I was one of them.

The first round seemed to go fine. I was in my usual, aggressive mode: not much defense and straight to the head. We exchanged punches and as I stepped in to move her toward the ropes, I was caught. I walked into her straight left. POW! I was down before I ever knew what hit me. My instinct had me up in no time, but I was not fully there. My mind told my body to punch, and I did. I was like a robot. I had no control of what I was doing. She continued her relentless attack on me. The ref thought he knew best and jumped in.

He threw his arms around me and said, "It's over Mia. It's over. You're OK."

He saved me because I never would have saved myself. The only solace came when my opponent couldn't bask in her glory because the crowd booed her. She was a black fighter who beat a Mexican in San Antonio and it was not the place to do it.

All I could do was cry on my way back to the dressing room. It was my first loss, and it was live on national television. My knockout would replay over and over again for anyone who may have missed it. I remember crying and looking up at Tony Ayala, who was the main event and notorious for his battles outside the ring instead of inside it. He said, "Everyone has their day in the ring. Today was just your day."

I had been working without a trainer for some time, bouncing around from gym to gym. When I returned home, I called Fernando Vargas, a professional boxer and the pride of Oxnard, a coastal town west of Los Angeles. He was a two-time light middleweight world champion and he directed me toward La Colonia, a barrio in the city's center that was created to house workers who worked at the nearby sugar factory and beet fields. There, I would find a gym with Eduardo and Roberto Garcia, a father-and-son powerhouse. Eduardo was Roberto's father and acted as a surrogate father to Fernando. The gym was small and rundown, but it was the heart of La Colonia, a place where dreams were made.

While Mexican migrants worked in the fields, many of their children went to the gym after school to train. They gym used to be a fire station. It was hot and reeked of sweat, but it was clean and had a feel to it that I had remembered from long ago. Ranchero music was blasting through the speakers and the usual sounds of the punching bag echoed through the gym. Roberto, who was known as "Grandpa," was training there. He helped out his father Eduardo, who did not speak English, nor did he care to learn. If I was going to train with him, I'd have to speak Spanish. My Spanglish was enough to get me by.

Together, Roberto and Eduardo worked on my technique. They transformed my wild swinging style and taught me defense. They taught me to move. They turned me into a boxer.

It was something no one had ever done before. I drove an hour there and back every day, but I found what I was looking for, a trainer who truly cared about his fighters. No one could replace Art, and I had accepted that at this stage in my career. Roberto became my main trainer so that Eduardo could devote his time to Fernando. Roberto soon retired from his own career as a fighter. We got along well. He knew what it felt like to walk in the ring and put your life on the line. He knew all the hard work that went into training, the torture of drying out, the constant ups and downs of the business. In short, he felt my pain, my fear, and my triumphs. I knew I would retire with him in my corner.

I ended up leaving the promoter I signed with and became an independent, free of any promoter or manager. I knew at this point in my career, I could take my name and book my own fights. I spoke directly to promoters, and basically sold myself to the highest bidder. I went to Dan Goossen and fought my next few fights on Fox Sports Net.

By this time, I was making less than I'd made with any promoter. I was sliding down the ladder. I didn't care. I just wanted to fight and I was still being televised, so I remained content. After compiling a few wins on my record, I went to Roberto and told him I wanted to fight Christy Martin.

Surprisingly, Roberto agreed. He believed in me more than I believed in myself. It was the encouragement I craved. I started to phone promoters and pitched the idea. I reached out to Christy and she started doing the same. She ended her partnership with Don King around the same time I ended mine with Arum. She was an independent, which meant we were free to fight who we wanted.

My main focus was my professional life for so long, I'd forgotten to work on my private life. I had gone through a string of short-lived love affairs throughout my career, but I was too obsessed with boxing to make any of them last. It didn't help that whoever I dated in my hometown usually ended up on the radio or television. I know I wasn't that famous, but I had a habit of meeting other athletes. Basically, we traveled in the same orbit. Without drugs and alcohol in my life, my true self was extremely shy and modest. It was difficult for me to ever approach anyone and get to know him. But in 2002, I met a major league baseball player who I'll call Jim.

I'd met him a few years before when he was in the minors. Now, he was all grown up and in his third year in the major leagues. We hit it off instantly. He was the son of a famous baseball player. He was extremely charismatic and down-to-earth, definitely different than the usual athletes I met. Jim was sincere and genuine. He instantly stole my heart. I can easily classify him as one of the great loves of my life. When the season started, Jim was signed by a team on the East Coast. He had been traded multiple times in his career, but he was excited for this one.

In February, he left for spring training in Florida. I spent a week with him and it was magical. Between boxing matches, I flew to be with him. We spent every moment we could together. It was hard being apart. After spring training, he was quickly traded to another Eastern team. I could hear the disappointment in his voice when he told me. I remembered telling him I'd visit him as soon as I could, and that I'd follow him to Egypt if I had to. I never had to travel that far, but I met him in Chicago, New York, and Baltimore every chance I could. Truth be told, these trips were always hard on me. It was difficult each time I said goodbye, but I always felt guilty when I wasn't working at my computer, searching for fights and endorsements. I was managing my own career and I had to do everything to be successful. It was a time-consuming job.

When I was with him, I'd workout, go to his game, and then I'd wait for him, sometimes more than three hours. It wasn't that bad. I enjoyed watching him play. In May, I flew to San Francisco to watch him play after one of my Fox Sports Net fights. This was a mistake.

I performed terribly and I was practically booed out of the ring for a fight that the crowd and commentators believed I should not have won. I hadn't shaken off the fight, and I flew to meet Jim the following day. You never want to be around any athlete who's consumed with their latest game. I was a complete bitch, and I could not wait to get back home. I was inconsolable and my mood could not be lifted. I needed to hurt someone and Jim was there in front of me.

When he left for his game, I took the next plane home to lick my wounds alone. We made plans to meet again in Baltimore, but as the date grew closer, the tension was palpable. He asked me not to visit because he needed to concentrate on his baseball. He had been in a slump for a while and was starting to come out of it. It put a strain on our relationship. I knew Jim had cheated on previous girlfriends, and I don't know why I thought he would be any different with me. I genuinely thought he would never cheat on me. On June 24, he forgot my birthday. On June 25, we made up and I flew out to see him in Baltimore.

Looking back, the clues were all there. They were bright red signs with blinking lights, but I ignored them. When I arrived, I knew in my heart he was cheating on me. Jim didn't cook and rarely ate at home, yet there was fresh lettuce in a Tupperware bowl in the fridge. There was a landline inside his home that I didn't know about. I heard it ring but I couldn't find the phone. He grew distant. The worst part was the sympathetic looks I got from the players' wives. They knew and so did I. We all did. By the end of the trip, I hated him. But I couldn't leave him. I hated myself for loving him.

I had to leave for Big Bear, a mountainous area east of Los Angeles, so I could train. There wasn't time to dwell on the state of our relationship. Still, I managed. Big Bear is isolated and can be very lonely, so I had plenty of time to drive myself crazy. What was he doing? Who was he with? Does he still love me? Is he thinking of me? It drove me mad. I couldn't eat and dropped nearly 15 lbs. I fought my next fight at 127 lbs., a weight I hadn't been for quite some time. This is even harder to do when you're on steroids. I had started taking steroids when I started thinking about fighting Christy. I had to put on the weight, and I decided it had to be muscle weight.

I was hesitant for a long time because I was afraid of the side effects. I thought I was defeating the purpose of training. The biggest contradiction was the desire to look strong and healthy while also being strong and healthy. Every athlete I knew was using them. Even female fighters. Athletes from every sport, man or woman, was using them. I couldn't blame anyone for using them. Athletes are in their thirties and forties and are expected to put bodies in stadium seats by performing at superhuman levels for the audience. Everyone wants home runs, knockouts, and touchdowns. Why does anyone care what we do to our bodies? It doesn't make you a better athlete, it just makes you a bit stronger and, perhaps, look better with less fat weight.

People say it's not fair to the other players. How do they know the other players aren't doing it also? Because they tested negative? The masking drugs are so good nowadays, you can't get caught unless you're one of the unlucky ones. A lot of the female fighters I've met use steroids. I don't care that I'm not on them anymore. I believe it didn't make me any better at my sport. It just made me very cranky. I grew facial hair and I had a complete loss of my sex drive. It made me physically harder, and I gained weight, but I looked bloated. I slowed down a lot because of the weight too. I stayed on them for almost three years. It was hard to give them up because I'd grown addicted to the look it gave me.

In the end, I was supposed to catch a plane to meet Jim, but before I left, I had a 6 a.m. TV interview. At 4:30 a.m., Jim called. He told me not to get on the plane. He was seeing someone else, he said. I was devastated. We agreed to talk later. I hung up the phone, but I knew I would never speak to him again. I cried all morning between takes in my trailer. I felt bad for the makeup artist and the director because I was a complete mess. I poured my heart out to my friends and to anyone who would listen. Jim called a few times after that day, but I refused to answer his calls. Instead, I changed all my numbers. I immersed myself into my training for my fight with Christy and never looked back.

The fight was scheduled for December 6, 2002, at the Silverdome in Pontiac, Michigan. I trained relentlessly and every time I thought of Jim, I pushed myself even harder. I would not date anyone for two years. I was completely celibate. My friends thought I had lost my mind. The steroids helped because I had no sexual desire whatsoever. The thought of being with a man was too much to handle. I never wanted to be hurt like that again.

The day finally arrived. I fought Christy Martin. It would be the biggest payday of my career. I sat in the dressing room waiting for that familiar knock. This time, it was different. I was fighting one of the greatest female fighters in the world, the woman who put women's boxing on the map, the girl who could pack a punch—the one everyone said would knock me out in the first round.

My heart was pounding in my throat, once again, and my legs were wobbly. My mom stood across from me holding a towel, the one she swore she would throw in the ring if Christy hurt her little girl. Everyone stood around me. I was scared.

For a moment, I thought to myself, "I could walk out of here and take the first plane home. What could they do?"

I remembered the moment six years earlier, when I sat in the same position with my beloved Art. It was my big chance, and we were so scared. All of my memories came flooding back. I remembered my debut fight for Don King. I remembered how we both laughed when I told him that one day I would open for Oscar De La Hoya and fight Christy Martin.

He smiled and said, "Let's get through this one, first."

If I could get through Christy, then I would have accomplished everything I set out to do. My only regret was that Art wasn't there to see it. This is what I'd been working for. I'd never known how good I was or wasn't. I had to know. Were the critics right? Was I not worthy of being in the ring with Christy Martin? I was determined to prove everyone wrong. I knew one thing for certain, Christy wouldn't underestimate me. The knock finally came. I looked at Fredia Gibbs, my sparring partner, and said, "I'm scared."

Fredia, a former champion, came with her words of wisdom and said, "Ain't nothing but a party baby, and tonight's your party." I was relieved she was there.

I walked through the tunnel to the ring. I remember thinking how surreal it was to have Christy Martin standing across the ring from me. I was excited and scared. We were given our instructions, then I turned to my corner and knelt down on one knee and said, "God be with me."

My strategy for the first few rounds was to feel her out and let her show me her moves. As I predicted, she tried to knock me out early. I saw the punches coming early enough to get out of the way. Just use my jab and study her from far away, I thought. I didn't feel any of her punches and it began to feel a little too easy. Maybe I had underestimated myself. As the rounds went on, I became bolder as I realized she couldn't hurt me. The baddest woman in boxing could not hurt me.

In the last rounds, I decided to go toe-to-toe to see what would happen. Before I knew it, ten rounds happened, and I wanted more. I could have gone twenty more. Sometimes, I forget I lost the fight. People come up to me and say, "Congrats on your victory." I smile and say thank you, forgetting that I lost.

I feel like I won. I feel like a winner, like every woman should who steps into the ring in front of them and conquers her fears. We train hard to face those fears. We all deserve respect for what we are willing to do. I once read a poster that said, "Only those who dare to lose, succeed." I will always have respect for Christy Martin. Without her, I wouldn't be where I am today, and women's boxing would not have come as far as it has. She gave me the opportunity to challenge myself and conquer my fear. As the final bell rang, I hugged her and said, "We did it, Christy! We really did it!" I am thrilled that I got the opportunity to live out one of my dreams.

I didn't get the decision I wanted, but I was victorious in so many ways.

It would be another ten years before she was willing to give me a rematch. In 2012, we fought for the WBC middleweight title. I had never been more prepared. My entire family came to the fight, including Kristoff, who was my biggest supporter. In Fresno, California, the Mexican flags were flying high that night as I made my entrance from the tunnel to the crowd. The roar of the fans was electrifying. My heart was beating loudly. I was overwhelmed with emotion, but I was confident. I had waited ten long years for this. The first few rounds started slowly, but by round four, I knew the fight was mine and I let her know it. With every ding of the bell, she grew more and more bewildered.

In the final round, she threw her hands down and quit fighting. I was confused, and so was everyone else. All of a sudden, a feeling rushed over me, a feeling that I'd never felt before in boxing: compassion.

I had two choices—keep pummeling her, or stop and risk the judges giving her the fight. I immediately stopped punching. Instead, I grabbed and held her until the bell rang. I knew a human life was more important than any belt. When all three judges announced me as the winner, I dropped to my knees and started crying. It was the greatest moment of my career. I had accomplished all of my goals. My mother was right, "What I think, I become."

I continued to fight for the WBC all across Mexico, and I was ultimately inducted into the National Boxing Hall of Fame. In 2017, I fought my last fight in New Zealand and left with a victory. But retirement was difficult and left me in a dark depression.

CHAPTER SEVEN

AFTER THE CHRISTY MARTIN FIGHT, I CONTINUED FIGHTING, BUT THE FIGHTS GREW FEWER AND FARTHER BETWEEN. Someone once told me it was like being a rock star—one day you're playing the Coliseum, and the next day you're performing in front of a few dozen people at Dino's Bar & Grill. I went from pay-per-view fights to ESPN to Fox Sports Net and finally satellite, if I was lucky. I never regretted the trajectory of my career because I accomplished everything I ever set out to do.

At the height of my career, Kristoff was doing most of the heavy lifting at home. He was an amazing father when the kids were little. He woke them up each morning, made sure they ate breakfast and dressed for school, always making sure they had everything they needed. I was always on the road, so there were a lot of bedtime phone calls between the kids and me. But as the kids got older, Kristoff became more of a disciplinarian. He wanted things done a certain way, and as the children began to grow into their personalities, it became more of a struggle.

Whenever I could bring the kids on the road with me, I would. After I won one of my five national titles, I took them to China. Like my dad did for me, I took them to museums and monuments. One of my favorite memories was watching my son Julian walk across The Great Wall. Julian was a sensitive soul who was developing into an artist and absorbed every new experience.

As Julian became a teenager, his mood began to change. I assumed he was being a typical teen, but for some reason, it didn't feel right. I worried that he might have inherited our genes. Both of his parents were alcoholics, after all. I started monitoring his mood swings, which could turn in an instant. He always denied he was drinking and I never smelled alcohol on his breath, so I believed him.

I still couldn't shake the notion that something was wrong. If anyone would've asked me, "What's your biggest fear as a parent?" I would've said having a child with schizophrenia.

I had a degree in psychology and had worked with many people of all ages struggling with the disease. I knew there was no cure and it was a lifelong degenerative illness. I tried making up excuses as I watched Julian withdraw from the world. As a child, he was diagnosed with attention deficit disorder. I assumed this is what happened to children as they grew older. He'd spend hours inside his room away from me and his father. I convinced myself that all teens acted like this.

When Julian was fifteen, he started drinking. He didn't try to hide it. I asked him what was wrong and why he thought he would find the answers in a bottle. I tried every tactic I knew to get him to stop. I tried talking to him about everything I had learned in my AA meetings. I yelled at him and tried to ground him. I hugged him and told him I understood. Nothing seemed to work. He just continued to grow more distant.

His depression was undeniable, and I took him to several doctors for help. Some doctors diagnosed him with Asperger syndrome; others said he was bipolar. Finally, I got the news I feared the most. He was diagnosed with paranoid schizophrenia. At first, I felt helpless and wondered what his life would be like. As a mother, all I want to do is protect my children so they can have a long and healthy life while experiencing joy and happiness. I wondered how I was going to make that happen for my only son.

At first, he was committed to taking his medication. He was a talented artist and I encouraged him to paint and draw. I had studied art in college, and I used the tools I learned to get him to express himself, especially when he felt like the medication took his personality away. He was extremely creative and talented. I know all parents say that about their kids, but Julian really was.

As I witnessed firsthand how important it was to detect mental health issues at an early age, I became involved in advocating for detecting mental health issues at school. I joined forces with Henry Acosta who was the executive director of the National Resource Center for Hispanic Mental Health. He introduced me to California congresswoman Grace Napolitano who was trying to pass the Mental Health in Schools Act, a bill that would provide funds for public schools to partner with mental health professionals to provide on-campus care for students.

I was invited to speak at a mental health summit in Washington, DC, where I spoke about my experience with trying to get help for my son. If there were licensed professionals on campus, perhaps my son would've been properly diagnosed at a younger age.

While I was traveling to DC advocating for better programs surrounding mental health, my son was spiraling into the depths of darkness. When Julian quit taking his medication, he'd become more and more aggressive. He never hurt me, but I could tell he came close to it. I never blamed him because I knew it was the illness inside his brain.

What most people didn't know was that my ex-husband was struggling with demons of his own. Kristoff was bipolar. He didn't consider it a mental illness. He thought he was in complete control of his moods. When he took his medication as prescribed, he would have long stretches of sobriety. But like a lot of patients, he didn't like the way he felt when he was medicated, so he'd quit taking them and replace them with the drugs of his choice. Every time he went out and used, he would miss work. He could disappear for days at a time. Executives from his show would force him into rehab, then check him out and send him back to work.

Meanwhile, I was searching the streets and walking through abandoned buildings looking for my son. And when I wasn't able to find him, I was at home crying and hoping I didn't get a call informing me my son was in a hospital, in jail, or worse. Once my son turned eighteen, I could never get the authorities to help me find him and bring him home. I traveled to some of the city's darkest places to find my son. One night, I found him inside a park bathroom. Next to him was a notebook. Once I got him back home, I started going through his notebook, which was filled with dozens of self-portraits drawn with blue ink, pencil, or anything he could get his hands on. My son was an artist and his work deserved to be seen.

I collected his drawings and showed them to a friend with connections to the art world. For a year, many of his paintings were shown at contemporary art spaces throughout Southern California. A friend of mine took Julian's portfolio and showed it to Shane Townley, the director of the Laguna Gallery of Contemporary Art. He said Julian exhibited "incredible raw talent" and gave him a one-night show called "The Art of Julian," which featured his drawing and paintings. The gallery described it as a "journey through psychosis."

Congresswoman Napolitano showed up to support my son. Julian's father was there and beamed all night as he talked about his son's talent. Julian may not have outwardly shown his excitement, but I could tell he loved sharing his feelings to the world. For a moment, we were a family, and my son was happy. It was a night I'll always remember.

CHAPTER EIGHT

JULIAN, OUR FIRST BORN AND ONLY SON, FOUND A PLASTIC TRASH BAG. I don't know why Julian became fixated with the plastic bag, but it was now his enemy. He'd taken the plastic bag and covered his head with it. He pulled it tight around his neck and started twisting the bottom tight like a twist tie in order to get rid of the excess air. It had only been about thirty seconds when a hospital attendant discovered him fighting his own instinct to breathe, but it was long enough for him to know that he could do it if given the opportunity. The attendant immediately called for help to remove the bag.

It was 2014, and Julian had been in a mental health rehabilitation center for about two months. His therapies had grown more difficult to maintain. Like many parents of children with mental health issues, our goal was to find help for our son who suffered from a horrific illness for which there is no cure. We knew that, with proper medication and therapy, Julian had a chance of living a comfortable life. After multiple stays at various rehabilitation hospitals across the country, we sought help from Los Angeles County's Department of Mental Health, which referred us to this particular facility. We had hoped that the facility would help him withdraw from meth and get him back on his meds, and that within the year, Julian would come home.

We made a fatal mistake placing our son in their care. The staff told us that our son, because of his suicidal behavior, would be checked every fifteen minutes. Yet, a little more than six weeks after he arrived, Julian escaped from the facility by climbing the fence. When I asked management and several of the employees how my son, who was supposed to be checked on regularly, could escape, they responded, seemingly unconcerned, "It happens."

Julian was missing for several hours before police found him at a bus stop. But in the days after he returned to the facility, Julian managed to smoke in the bathroom and even consume alcohol. Then, five days after he escaped, Julian attempted suicide using a plastic bag. His roommate discovered him and alerted the staff. I was terrified to leave Julian there, but staffers vehemently assured me that plastic bags would be banned from the section of the facility where he lived, and Julian would never be left alone. But after about two weeks, he was taken off twenty-four-hour watch and put back on fifteen-minute precautionary watch.

He was addicted to meth, his current drug of choice, and I was hoping the hospital could help him detox. He had been suicidal while off his medication. The staff upgraded him to a fourteen-day hold and lengthened it for an indefinite period to give him adequate time to get off meth. We'd been in a bad cycle and I needed them to help us get out of it. It had been the same for a while.

He was living with me and for a short time, everything would be calibrated and running smoothly. He was sober and taking his meds like clockwork. I was a helicopter mom and always hovering over him, making sure he took his meds on time. These moments of peace were never long enough. Just because he took his medication didn't mean his mind was at peace. He had schizophrenia and the voices in his head were always there, but the medication helped keep them at a distance. They weren't as dangerous as they could be, or they had been. But eventually, the voices would start to creep closer, and Julian would run away.

He wasn't ever running away from me, but it always seemed he was trying to get ahead of the voices. In his own way, he was protecting me, keeping the voices away from me and our house. The voices were unwanted visitors and Julian knew it. When he ran away from home, he'd leave his medicine behind. In order to quiet the noise in his head, he'd self-medicate. This is where the meth came in.

He'd do anything to get his hands on some meth and once he did, the smoke would swirl in his head and blanket all of his emotions with a thick haze. He'd become disoriented and start wandering the streets of Los Angeles. I never got an answer for where he was going, but I always knew he was trying to get away. He always disappeared for a few days at a time.

While he was missing, I'd be in panic mode, crazily searching for him. I cried all the time. As hours turned to days, I worried and wondered where he might be. I couldn't eat or sleep. I never felt angry, but I often felt utter despair and was frightened. I had bouts of self-pity and I'd ask, "Why me? Why my son?"

It just felt like a never-ending saga. There was never a moment where I felt good in the morning. Instead, I'd wake up feeling anxious and scared of what could possibly happen to my son that day. Is he going to the streets to use? Is he going to get arrested like he often did? Is he going to end up dead? Every day was like that. Every day, I lived in fear with my stomach in knots. Every day, I was scared to death. Every single day.

The worry consumed me, and it would continue to build. If I was going to get any rest, I needed to see Julian with my own eyes and hear him with my own ears. It was then that I'd start looking for him in the usual places. I'd start visiting the jails to see if he'd gotten into trouble, I'd visit the nearby hospitals to see if he'd been hurt, I'd check under the trees at different parks to see if he was sleeping. I'd go everywhere looking for my child. I'd finally find him. Whenever I did, I'd give him the biggest hug and he'd hug me back. He was still my baby boy.

I'd give him a blanket and take him home, where I helped him get sober and back on his medication. Until the next time he ran away. It was like the movie *Groundhog Day*. Every day was the same. The routine never changed except for the length of time between searches. At this point, it felt like our lives were on a never-ending loop. We needed help. Julian was discovered in the street trying to jump in front of an oncoming truck. He was on meth and trying to commit suicide. He was 5150'd, a code for patients taken and checked into a facility against their will.

His father was upset with him. Kristoff didn't believe in mental illness. He thought it was something weak people made up to make themselves feel better. Kristoff had endured so much in his own life and thought he had a handle on it, so the idea that someone else couldn't handle their troubles was foreign to him. He thought our son needed tough love. He thought Julian needed to toughen up. It was an old-school philosophy, but Kristoff did not know any other way to be.

He was very mad at Julian and he'd say, "You need to get off your ass, and you've got to do this!"

He was heartbreakingly tough. He was tough to the point where it was really hurtful to Julian. Kristoff didn't understand his son was ill. When Julian tried to kill himself, the hospital called to tell us. I got to the hospital as quickly as I could. I needed to hug my son once more and tell him that everything was going to be okay. I wanted him to know that I needed him. Kristoff did not go to the hospital.

He told me, "No. I'm not going to see him. I'm not even going to talk to him." He said, "His punishment is my silence. He will receive no communication from me because I can't believe he pulled a stunt like that. He needs to get off his ass and stop feeling sorry for himself."

I tried to explain to Kristoff that our son was ill.

I kept saying, "Kristoff, he has schizophrenia. Don't you understand? He's hearing voices. The voices are telling him to kill himself."

Kristoff refused to hear me.

He said, "It's just a bunch of bullshit, and he just did it for attention. He really wasn't going to kill himself. He just wanted the attention."

I didn't have the time or desire to focus on Kristoff. How can you argue with someone who believes this about their own son? I had to save my energy for Julian.

It was a little before noon on a Sunday when Julian called me. Thanksgiving was in a few days and my daughter and I were running errands, checking things off our list for the big holiday. Julian was getting a twenty-four-hour pass from the hospital so he could spend the holiday with us. We still hadn't decided if we were going to have Thanksgiving at Kristoff's house in Los Angeles, or if we were all going to spend it at my house in Palm Springs. Regardless, we were all going to be together.

Despite all of our differences, Kristoff and I always remained friends. But we were more than that. We were soulmates, but not like it's portrayed in the movies. We were embedded in each other's souls. We shared two beautiful children and we knew each other better than anyone. We just couldn't live together or be married anymore. But we were each other's family. We planned on coming together for Thanksgiving.

On the guest list was Paris and her boyfriend, my son Julian, Kristoff, his mom, and whoever my ex-husband was dating at the time. We were all going to be there. Thanksgiving was a time for family, and we were a tight-knit crew that needed to be together. We still hadn't decided if we were going to order our meal or if I was going to cook. We all knew if Kristoff ordered the meal, we were going to have to eat on our own before or after dinner because we'd be starving.

Kristoff grew up a vegan, so if he was in charge, he'd order the most horrific, disgusting turkey, which wasn't even a turkey. It was like a rubber wannabe bird. It was so awful, but we never wanted to tell him. We would just push our food around the plate and make faces at each other when Kristoff wasn't looking. Even the worst meal was fun for me because we were together. The holidays were special for us and a time to celebrate our family, so we were looking forward to being a family once again.

I called Julian. He answered on the hospital's pay phone. There was only one phone on his floor and the patients took turns using it. When he was at the hospital, I was chained to my phone because I never wanted to miss his call. I was never far from it. I slept with it. I took a shower with it. It was always within reach.

So, when he called on November 23, 2014, I was driving and immediately grabbed it. His voice sounded funny. He was not in a good place. He told me the voices had changed. They were darker and meaner, he said.

Normally, the voice in his head belonged to someone else. It's hard to understand if you've never worked with people who are schizophrenic, but for my son, the voices in his head belonged to someone else. He'd fight them off, often telling them to go away or to leave him alone. For people diagnosed with schizophrenia, the voices are crystal clear. I was the only person Julian ever trusted, so when I told him they weren't real, he believed me. It helped him differentiate reality from the world inside his head.

But now, things had changed. He told me the voice was him. Basically, he was telling himself that he was a joke, and the joke was on him. I kept trying to tell him that the voice was in his head and he was talking to himself. Looking back, I regret telling him this. Usually, I could talk him out of a dark place because he always believed me. I told him that the voices were not real. In hindsight, I wish I'd told him to fight the voice and tell it to fuck off or, at the very least, to just shut it up. Instead, I told him not to believe it. I remember getting really depressed that he was so depressed.

Finally, my daughter got on the phone and tried to shine some of her sunlight onto him.

She told him, "I miss you. I want to come see you." Her voice was sweet and calming like a song. She had a way of cheering all of us up.

After a few moments, I got back on the phone with Julian and reminded him that he would be home in three days.

I told him, "We're coming to get you and we're going to spend Thanksgiving together."

He was looking forward to it. Both he and I knew that he wouldn't being going back to the hospital. He'd been there long enough. I would have never sent him back because I just couldn't. Once he was home, he was out. And so I knew he was really looking forward to the Wednesday before Thanksgiving. He even told his grandmother that he was coming home on Wednesday. He'd told her earlier that day. He said he needed to go, and I told him I'd talk to him later.

My daughter and I had been in my car, sitting in the driveway while we spoke to Julian. After we hung up, she ran inside because she had forgotten something.

When she got back in the car, she said, "He's really depressed. Call him back."

I told her to wait and to give him a minute to calm down and collect his thoughts. Paris was emphatic that I call him back. Reluctantly, I called, and a strange voice answered the phone.

"Is Julian there?" I asked.

The unfamiliar voice said he couldn't come to the phone and hung up.

Paris looked at me and said, "Call him back! Call him back!"

I hesitated because I didn't want to be the pushy mom that I usually was. I was always ready with a freak out. Kristoff would tell me, "You're always ready to call 911. There's always a fire alarm going off." I always panicked and freaked out if Julian wasn't doing well. But for some reason, this time, I thought, "Let's be calm. Let's give him a minute and see what happens."

I was in very good shape at the time. Exercise was my savior during my most difficult moments. It allowed me to clear my head so that I had the strength and energy to handle anything that came my way. In Palm Springs, there's a three-and-a-half-mile stretch of road that leads you to the Aerial Tram. It's an incredibly steep hill that increases in elevation. It's quite a challenge, but one that I did often. Paris and I headed to the area and started our workout. As I raced up the hill, I remember saying, "I can't breathe. I can't breathe," which was very unusual for me. When we got to the top, we took a photo with the picturesque views of the Coachella Valley behind us. I was in fighting shape, but I simply didn't feel good.

As we headed home, the hospital's director called me. As soon as I picked up, she asked, "Are you driving?" I said yes and she asked, "Do you want to call me back?"

I immediately sensed something was wrong and was screaming when I asked, "Is there something wrong with my son?"

She asked me again, "Are you driving?"

I couldn't believe it. I told her to tell me what was wrong, and she said I needed to call her back when I wasn't driving.

I just started screaming, "You're going to tell me now. Tell me what happened to my son. What happened to my son? What's wrong?"

She said that Julian had passed. I couldn't quit screaming. I have no idea how I didn't wreck my car. I just couldn't accept what she was telling me. It wasn't real. There was nothing real about what she was saying. And I just kept screaming.

I tried calling Kristoff over and over. It was Football Sunday and he wasn't answering his phone. He liked spending the day alone watching games all day. He'd surround himself with bowls of chips and popcorn. He would drink all day, yelling and cheering for his teams. He was a Los Angeles Raiders fan, but he loved watching all the games. It was as if his entire day was a cheat day, and he liked being left alone. But I kept calling and calling and he wouldn't pick up.

Finally, he answered. "What, Mia?" he asked, his voice filled with exasperation.

I couldn't say a word. I was just wailing into the phone. He knew. It's like he knew right then what had happened. I didn't even have to say a word. I was screaming. I just kept saying Julian's gone.

Kristoff was in Los Angeles, so he headed straight to the hospital. He ran so fast out of his house that he tripped and hurt himself. But he didn't care. He told me later that he was yelling the minute he broke through the hospital's metal doors. My trip to the hospital remains a blur. My daughter's boyfriend at the time came over to my house and drove all of us to Los Angeles. On a good day, it takes about an hour and forty-five minutes to get from Palm Springs to Los Angeles. I think we got there in about an hour. We just raced through the desert.

As soon as I got there, I ran up the steps and barreled through the doors of the lobby and started screaming, "You killed my son! You killed my son!"

I was throwing anything that wasn't bolted down. I pulled everything off the walls. I was angry and wanted someone to feel the pain I was feeling at the moment. My daughter's then-boyfriend, who was 6'4" and very strong and muscular, wrapped his arms around me and ushered me out the doors. He knew I needed to get out of there. He knew I wanted to go into that place with a machine gun and take out everyone. Immediately, I was dead set on revenge. I had so much anger in my heart and I didn't know what to do with it. Where was I supposed to direct all of my anger?

It was a shitty investigation. We'll never really know what happened to my son. Before that day, Julian had been telling his dad and me that his roommate was going to kill him. His roommate was a very large guy, more than six feet tall and about 280 lbs. It was like having a football player at the hospital, roaming the corridors. His roommate had a long history of mental illness and criminal activity. But when you're in the hospital, it seems like that's everyone story and you figure everyone is safe because the doctors are supposed to be monitoring everyone's mental health.

I eventually got the surveillance video from that day. At first, it was like watching a dream. I watched my beautiful Julian approach the pay phone and speak to me. Then, I watched Julian hang up the pay phone after our last conversation together. As I continued to watch, a pit grew deep in my stomach because I knew what was going to happen. My dream was turning into a nightmare in front of my eyes, in a silent black-and-white video. I wanted it to stop. Maybe if I stopped watching, I could somehow prevent the inevitable. But I needed to see what happened to my baby.

Julian walked to his room and shut the door. Shortly after, his roommate followed him and closed the door behind him. The video showed his roommate walk out of their room, shut the door, and walk toward the pay phone where he took the receiver off the hook and walked away. It was incredibly surreal watching this, knowing that your son is dying off camera. I started screaming at the video for someone to help my son.

About forty-five minutes later, an attendant walked into my son's room to check on him. They found him face down on the bathroom floor with a bag over his head and bruises on his face. The hospital staff promised me they were going to get rid of every single plastic bag, but they didn't because when Julian finally did take his life, he used the same bag. These bags are now prohibited from suicide units.

Every forensic scientist will tell you that you can't die with a bag over your head because your reflex is going to yank the bag off when you can't breathe. You have to be on a sedative or something. His toxicology report showed that Julian did not have any drugs in his system. We don't know what happened in that room.

The Long Beach Police Department didn't investigate my son's case. They just ruled it a suicide. I was livid. I said, "How could you do that to my son?"

And they said, "Well, ma'am, do you know how many deceased young adult black males come across our desk every day?"

The hospital was on the border of Long Beach and Compton, so there were a lot. As a result, they didn't put too much thought or care into it. They didn't have the resources or time. Finally, they said something like, "We didn't know he was your son"—as if it mattered whose child he was. No one should have to endure what we endured.

Through my own investigation, I know they neglected my child because the whole hour that they were supposed to be checking on him, since he was on suicide watch, they were writing in the hospital's notes, "Julian's eating lunch," and "Julian's watching TV." Employees recorded that they checked on Julian every fifteen minutes, as mandated. The sickening insult is that their records showed the staff performing the mandatory checks on Julian dutifully until 3:15 p.m. My son was already dead and taken out of the facility by approximately 1:30 p.m.

The facility claimed that staffers attempted to save Julian's life, but according to 911 tapes and the Long Beach Police Department, no one from the facility called for emergency assistance until seventeen minutes after he was found. From the second the director called me, I knew I was not going to let the hospital, or any other entity involved in the death of my son, off the hook. I was coming after them. That's who I am. I wasn't just a fighter in the ring, I was a fighter, period. The hospital neglected my son. They falsified his record. And I was going to come after them.

I don't remember much about Julian's funeral. I spent most of the time in shock. I do remember that I wore a black dress I found in the back of my closet. I put it on and wore it with a stone-cold expression, the same one I'd seen my mother wear so many years before. Kristoff made it as beautiful as possible and everyone from *The Young and the Restless* attended. I know people were shocked that I wasn't crying. The idea that my child had died was unfathomable. I couldn't believe it. I wouldn't believe it. I looked at everybody else and thought, "Why are they crying? My son's not gone. There's no way. This did not happen." Because if I had let myself go there, I would have been hospitalized.

Eventually, I was, but at that moment, I went back to saying, "No, this is not real. My son is here, and it's just a matter of me finding him and then I can go on with my day."

For a long while after the funeral, it wasn't good between Kristoff and me. I blamed him for Julian's death. He should've done more to support him, I thought. It was his fault that Julian was addicted to meth. Kristoff should have believed our son had a mental illness. It was Kristoff's fault that my baby boy was gone. I soon realized that Kristoff was thinking the exact the same thing. I learned that Kristoff didn't realize Julian was ill until he took his life. "Oh my God. I was wrong. He is ill," Kristoff eventually told me.

After an immense amount of therapy, I learned to forgive Kristoff. I attended countless support groups, anywhere I could unload the burden of my pain and others could relate to the grief I carried. These organizations saved me. I knew it wasn't Kristoff's fault that our son was gone. I just needed to blame someone, and it was easy to blame him.

I soon learned that even though I forgave Kristoff, he never forgave himself. Kristoff and I dealt with Julian's death completely differently. He drowned himself in drugs and alcohol, and I stayed sober. I knew that if I ever used, I would die. People often ask me, "Well, do you feel a sense of relief now that he's gone?" and the answer is no. No, no, no. When you're a parent, when you're a mother, you would still rather be in the worst situation imaginable, as long as your child is alive. I always knew that. I prayed every night, "Please God, protect my son. Protect my son. Never take my son from me. Never take him from me. I will gladly deal with this every day of my life for the rest of my life, just don't take my son."

And I said that every single night. I was there when Julian came into this world and I should have been there when he left. It was the worst day of my life and will forever be the worst day of my life. Some days, I still can't accept that he's gone. I know there's a way to find my son, because he's somewhere. And I'll live for the rest of my life trying to find him.

CHAPTER NINE

AFTER A LOT OF INTENSE THERAPY, I REALIZED KRISTOFF WASN'T THE REASON JULIAN PASSED AWAY. Part of my healing included apologizing to Kristoff and telling him I loved him. I'm grateful I did, but Kristoff continued to carry a lot of guilt.

Still, I was devastated after the death of my son. That devastation turned into anger and I needed someone in my corner who could be as angry as me. I wanted a lawyer who could kick some serious ass, someone with power. Kristoff came to me with the idea of going to so called "celebrity" attorney, Mark Geragos. I didn't know much about him except he had handled some very high-profile cases: Michael Jackson, Chris Brown, and Scott Peterson, among many others. I was steadfast against hiring Mark.

I thought he was too big for our case and wouldn't give my son the attention he deserved. I was determined to destroy the hospital that caused my son's death and I needed someone who could fight alongside me.

Kristoff fervently believed he was the right guy for us. After much persuasion, Kristoff was able to get me to agree to go see and meet Mark. When we arrived at his downtown office in Los Angeles, I realized he didn't just own an office, or even a few floors. He owned the entire building! It was an older, elegant building that was very tastefully decorated. Before even getting into the elevator, I was greeted by security who made a call to the top to make sure I was scheduled and expected. Mark is so mysterious, I recalled. I found myself intrigued. His assistants looked more like models on a runway rather than stressed-out paralegals. When I first walked into his office, he was intimidating. Mark has a strong presence, but at the same time makes you feel at ease with his charm if he likes you. If he doesn't, he will let you know in a subtle way that he is not to be messed with. I guess we're very much alike in that sense. Mark was handsome, smart, charming, powerful—and he knew it. Mark Geragos knew exactly who he was and that's what I needed in an attorney.

I told him about my son Julian and the facility's negligence, the lack of monitoring, the mistakes in his medication, the falsifying of records and the so-called doctors who were rarely on-site. It was going to be a long process, Mark told us, but he agreed to help. I was sold on him at that first meeting, and we hired him on the spot. That started what turned out to be around-the-clock work like nothing I had ever done before. We were looking for anything and everything that might be helpful. We eventually obtained surveillance to prove all of our suspicions, which became the basis for our accusations.

I started digging into records and when they weren't readily available, I began filing requests through the Freedom of Information Act, a law that requires the U.S. government to disclose information or documents not previously released. Every citizen has the right to file and request the information. I discovered the facility had numerous violations and deaths that hadn't been revealed. The Department of Health tried to deny my requests, but I started a public pressure campaign by posting on Twitter. The records were eventually released to me. I called other parents of children who'd lost their children at the same facility. One family had just settled a lawsuit before Julian arrived. The more I learned about the facility's lack of transparency and shady practices, the more determined I became to get justice for my son and other families.

Mark and I hit it off immediately. We got along from the beginning. I knew he was a flirt, but I didn't care. My attraction to him was instant. Throughout the lawsuit,

Mark and I became extremely close but always maintained a professional relationship. Not only were we friends, but at times, he also became my therapist as I cried, kicked, and screamed for justice. He was constantly trying to pull in the reins but with little success. I would remind him that I was a mother. I also reminded him that I was a five-time world champ and kicking ass is what I did, and I was good at it. Mark understood me very well. He still, to this day, calls me his hero. What intrigued me about his style was that he approached life like a game of chess and he just knew how to play chess better than me. So, I listened and took his advice—on occasion! Throughout the lawsuit, I waged a war with the mental health facility through the media. I made sure this company never forgot who I was. I spoke to *People*, *Us Weekly*, *Entertainment Weekly*, and even wrote an op-ed in *The Washington Post*. Mark supported me through all of it. The hospital would eventually be found guilty of neglect and falsifying records. We settled on an undisclosed amount. I was grateful, but there wasn't enough money on the planet to ever make us feel like we got justice.

In addition to me, Mark was a good friend to Kristoff. Sure, Kristoff and Mark had their occasional battle of the egos, but it was because they both passionately cared. It was overwhelming at times to watch two of the most important men in my life fighting for justice. This kind of support kept me going through some of my darkest days.

Unfortunately, Kristoff was handling the loss of Julian much differently.

Kristoff was growing more and more despondent. It seemed like anyone who knew him had a story about finding Kristoff at home in a drunken stupor, disheveled and crying, on the verge of what looked like death. In those dark days, it was rare to find him for any period of time in a sober state. Since Julian's passing, those benders became more and more frequent. We'd all taken turns caring for Kristoff—his coworkers, his friends, his second ex-wife, our daughter, and me.

During his darkest days, he met a young Russian woman who appeared not to be interested in helping him. I discovered they traveled to Paris, France, when I saw a selfie of the two of them posted on Instagram. The sad look in his eyes told me everything. The problem was he failed to let anyone know he was traveling, including his employers. They demanded that he return to work, or he'd be fired. He returned, but the threats and ultimatums were hardly working. He just didn't care anymore.

Toward the end of January of 2019, it was my turn to take care of Kristoff. He was scheduled to appear on CBS's *The Talk*. It wasn't even 10 a.m. and he'd already been drinking. Unable to drive himself, I got him into the car and tried to sober him up on the way there. We talked about all of the things he would talk about on the show. He was a pro. He'd spent a lifetime having good days and bad days, and on those bad days, he was always able to clean up and turn it on for however long it was required. No one was ever the wiser. We arrived at the studio, and luckily, I was able to get him through makeup and the rundown of the show. He was wobbling and shaking. When he spoke, it was obvious he was intoxicated. He wasn't fooling anyone anymore. It broke my heart to watch him.

As we sat in the makeup room, he looked at me and laughed, "Aww Mia, here we are all these years later, together again. Look at us."

We sat backstage waiting for the green light, which meant taping had started. Kristoff was swaying and his eyes kept closing. Everyone noticed and the looks of concern were turned in my direction. Seconds later, Kristoff collapsed. He completely blacked out. When he regained consciousness, everyone debated whether he should soldier on. It didn't take long for Kristoff to decide the show must not go on after all. I drove him home and put him to bed. I stared at him while feeling helpless, knowing we were nearing the end. My beautiful Kristoff, he only wanted to see his baby boy. It was all too much.

A week later, Y&R co-stars Bryton James and Daniel Goddard went to Kristoff's house, where they found him drunk, once again. Daniel called me to tell me, and he didn't have to explain much. I knew exactly how Kristoff looked and how he was acting. We'd all seen it before, but now, it was never-ending. I told Daniel I could not come this time. They called Mark and he got on the phone with Kristoff.

Like I said earlier, Mark could be a real charmer. I don't know how he did it, but he was the only one able to get Kristoff to agree to check into a hospital. Finally, I thought. Kristoff was going to get better. They labeled him as an emergency, and he was taken to Las Encinas in Pasadena. He was placed on a 5150, an involuntary hold because authorities determined he was a danger to himself or others.

They held him for seventy-two hours and released him against my wishes, and Mark's as well. Mark told me he regretted not doing something more to ensure Kristoff remained in the hospital. We couldn't find Kristoff for two days, until he called me at about 11 a.m., two days later on Super Bowl Sunday.

My relationship with Mark continues to this day. We are confidantes and friends. I have spent a long time grieving. He has an office in New York and whenever I'm there, we always try to make time for a meal, or a laugh. If there is any silver lining to this nightmare, our relationship is one.

CHAPTER TEN

EVERY DAY, FROM MORNING TO NIGHT, IT GREW HARDER TO WATCH KRISTOFF. I knew in my heart he wasn't coming back from this because it was so bad. He was in a drunken stupor, taking pills day after day. He didn't care about anything. He couldn't care for the kids anymore and he couldn't care for himself. He told me multiple times he wanted to die. He wanted to be with his son, and nothing else mattered.

On the morning of Feb. 3, 2019, Kristoff and I were texting back and forth.

He wrote: Understand, you've got to live in the present observe all the good things in your life and others around you. Julian would not want you to live your life with bitterness and upset, it eats away with you and drains your life slowly but surely. You must rise to the occasion and accept the beauty around you. I believe in you.

I wasn't sure if he was writing these texts to me or for himself. It was about 11 a.m. when he called. I heard the helplessness in his voice as soon as I answered his call.

"Mia, thank God you answered," he said. He was slurring his words and he kept repeating that he didn't want to be here anymore. I could tell I was losing him, and I pleaded with him to stay with me a little longer. It was as if we'd been holding hands for more than thirty years, since the first day we met, and he was beginning to let go.

I started listing all the reasons he had to live. I reminded him about his work. He'd been an actor on the CBS soap opera for twenty-eight years. Few things brought him more joy than playing Neil Winters, which won him several Daytime Emmys. He loved going to work and hanging out with his work family, but he was no longer interested. I told him we could call his girlfriend, the Russian woman he'd been traveling with around the world. I didn't like her, but I was desperate. Maybe he'd perk up at the thought of seeing her again, but he wasn't interested. Finally, I brought up our daughter Paris, and his daughter Lola, whom he shared with his ex-wife. He said, "Call Lola. Call Paris. Tell them I love them."

He told me he loved me. "I love you. I always have. Do you still love me?" he asked.

I said, "I will always love you." And I meant it.

He cried and cried. He couldn't stop. Looking back, I think he was dying when he was on the phone with me.

I was scheduled to sign autographs at a sports expo that day. I told him I'd cancel and go over to be with him.

He said, "No, no, no. It's okay. It's okay. Julian's at the door. Julian's here."

As soon as he said that, I knew I was never going to see him again. We'd each grieved our son's passing differently—I was fighting through the pain and Kristoff was giving up.

I started screaming at him to stay with me when he said, "He's just going to take me for a walk."

I immediately panicked and hung up. I called his best friend Mark and told him he had to get over to Kristoff's.

He told me he didn't have a key to get inside, but I told him I didn't care. "Get over there and break down the door!"

The clock was ticking. I could feel it.

Mark called Kristoff's second ex-wife who lived nearby and had a key to his place. When they got inside Kristoff's house, it was too late. My Kristoff was gone.

When I walked inside his home, there were tons of people—his mother, his second ex-wife, and his friend who found him. We called his ex-girlfriend, the one before the Russian woman, so it was a full house of people crying. I can't remember if I was crying. I do remember every emotion—shock, disappointment, fear, and anger. I was angry that he'd left me here alone. He was a major part of my life. We shared two beautiful children together. If he was here, then a part of Julian was here with me. But now, he was with Julian. He was always going to be with Julian. They were going to be together forever. They were going to take walks together, laugh together, sit in the sun together—all of the things that I wanted to do. Instead, I was left behind with the pain and an aching in my heart that still remains. At that moment, I wanted to die so I could be with them.

I don't remember much after he died. My memories are like photographs seared into my mind. There's the one of me walking into Kristoff's home and seeing him on the floor. My next memory is at his funeral. It was beautiful and I know he would've loved it. There were dozens of people around me but I can't remember any of their faces. And finally, there's another memory of me strapped to a gurney, being checked into a hospital. At that point, I'd lost everything: my beautiful son, my best friend, and thirty years of sobriety. For six months, I'd been swimming in a pool of unbearable grief and pain.

Everyone thinks it's a monumental moment when you fall off the wagon, like something out of the movies, but it's not. In fact, I don't remember going to the store and I don't remember questioning whether it was a good idea. I just knew that I didn't want to feel what I was feeling. I drank every day after Kristoff passed. I wanted to do anything to escape the pain.

I have another memory from that time of me passed out on the floor of my boyfriend Larry's living room. There were a lot of people looking over me and someone was checking my pulse. The paramedics placed me in an ambulance and took me to the hospital.

I checked out of the hospital, but the entire scenario quickly happened again. This time, I was placed on a 5150. Somehow, I managed to locate my phone and I tweeted, "#ImNotCrazy I just lost my beautiful boys is there no compassion anymore??" Everyone was concerned. Strangers called my attorney and told him that I was being held against my will. It was true, but the hospital was supposed to. I was a threat to myself. My intention was to do what Kristoff did—just keep drinking until I died.

But I was released after seventy-two hours. One night, I threw myself the biggest pity party after Larry and I, who'd been together six years, called it quits. It wasn't the most significant event of my life, but it was the final jab capable of knocking me out after a series of painful blows.

When I think about that night, I have another snapshot in my brain. I'm sitting on the carpeted floor in my living room. I am surrounded by empty bottles of wine and Grand Marnier. Mascara is running down my face because I can't quit crying. I'm waiting to pass out, but before I can, I go to the bathroom and make myself throw up. It's a pathetic sight that occasionally flashes across my mind at unexpected moments. It makes me cringe, but it also reminds me that I don't want to be like this again.

After spending four days in a drunken stupor that I can't even remember, I woke up with clarity. I reminded myself of everything I've accomplished throughout my life and everything I've had to overcome. I thought about Julian and thought about what he would say if he saw me like this. I thought about my daughter, who was also grieving for the loss of her brother and her father. I knew I had taken my last drink. It was over. The pain from losing my son, his father, my boyfriend, and my sobriety would have to be dealt with head on.

Several studies show that 40 to 60 percent of addicts and alcoholics relapse within a year of their recovery. The longer you're sober, the more likely you are to sustain your recovery. But what if you've been sober for a decade or two? Or three? There are fewer studies surrounding long-term relapse and recovery. I was sober for thirty years before I relapsed. I knew the program: attend meetings, call a sponsor, get counseling, help others. It was easy to take for granted. There were times that I wondered if I was even an alcoholic because it had been so long. Let me be the first to tell you that if you're an alcoholic, you will always be an alcoholic. I am an alcoholic, but I'm committed to my sobriety and I'm determined to be successful.

CHAPTER ELEVEN

I STARTED GOING BACK TO AA MEETINGS, I HAVE THE HELP OF A DOCTOR, AND I MEDITATE CONTINUOUSLY. Sobriety does not happen overnight. I have bad days and I have really good days. I'm on the path to recovery.

For the longest time, anger was my driving force. When I woke up each morning, I used to think about how I was going to destroy the hospital that killed my son and dismantle the system that failed my ex-husband. I'm still determined to hold these facilities accountable and make them transparent, not because I'm on a quest for revenge but because it's the right thing to do.

I've been a fighter for most of my life. It's the core of who I am. I don't think I'd still be here if I wasn't. It took years, more like decades, to learn that my purpose wasn't achieved when I became a professional boxer. I am more than someone whose job was to brutally beat another human being. When I stepped into a ring, I was willing to kill my opponent for the sport, and I was willing to die for it. I risked my life each night for the thrill of competition and a paycheck. I like to think I evolved. I'm lucky to realize that boxing gave me a platform to find my true calling. I use my voice for all of the children who've died inside psychiatric hospitals, and I lend my voice to their parents who don't have access to a national audience. Everyone deserves to be heard.

I had no idea when I chose to study psychology that it would play such a huge role in my life. My degree in psychology, along with my own experience with mental health and addiction, has allowed me to speak at universities across the country, and in front of congressional committees about the disease. In 2008, I created El Saber Es Poder Foundation, which means knowledge is power.

It's a phrase my mother used to say and I'm glad she was able to see me create a nonprofit dedicated to empowering people suffering from mental illness, homelessness, addiction, and poverty by providing programs and tools to inform and improve their physical and mental health. She was able to witness my foundation, along with Micron, donate a computer lab with thirty computers, the internet, and electricity to el Barrio de la Cantera in Zacatecas, Mexico, the village where my mother and her family lived. It felt good to give back to a culture that gave me life.

Unfortunately, my mother passed away in June 2011, a few years before my son. My mother was in Mexico burying my uncle when she felt ill. My mother rarely got sick, and even though my sister had to rush her to the hospital, we all assumed she'd be okay.

Instead, doctors diagnosed her with stage IV lung cancer. We were shocked, especially since she wasn't a smoker. We tried everything to save her—chemotherapy, diet, meditation, and acupuncture. Nothing seemed to help, and the cancer only grew more aggressive.

She passed away on December 27, my father's birthday. Losing my mother was devastating, yet somehow acceptable. We are supposed to lose our parents, but we are not supposed to bury our children. When Julian passed away, I missed her more than ever. She wasn't here so I could cry on her shoulder, she wasn't here to tell me everything would be okay. She wasn't here to show me how to survive. If anyone could have helped me navigate through that insurmountable grief, it would have been my mother. She was the strongest person I ever knew.

For months, I walked through a fog. I finally hit rock-bottom, as they say, and like many times throughout my life, I got back up to fight. I hope my story shows people that it's possible to survive life's darkest moments.

It may be a challenge, but it's indeed possible. Each step taken to maintain a sober life includes helping others. It's like a boomerang: when you're kind to others, it will come back to you. The more you give, the more you will receive.

I took my own advice to heart a week after becoming sober and reached out to my father. As complicated as our relationship is, I love him, and I wanted him to know. I've seen him less than a handful of times in my life, but if I wanted to forgive myself, I knew that I needed to forgive him. We have a long way to go before we have a positive relationship, but I've chosen to get rid of my anger and that makes me happy.

Our daughter Paris, now twenty-nine, has suffered so much from losing her brother and father, and then me, to the depths of grief and alcoholism. I wanted so much to be there for her, but I was suffering too much to be her parent. It was foreign to her to see her mother in a drunken stupor and fighting her for the keys to my car. It was an image she'd never seen or experienced because she'd grown up with a sober mom.

She and Julian were only two years apart, yet they were almost inseparable. It seemed as though she lost her other half. We struggled through grief therapy together—she was the stronger one. It was as though our roles were reversed. She became the parent and I was the child. There was nothing more demoralizing for me.

She was extremely talented, like her father, and was attending Berklee College of Music in Boston for her singing and piano playing. Julian took his life when she was home for a school break, and she made the decision not to go back. She spiraled into a deep depression.

It felt like our worlds came to a screeching halt. But I found strength in her. She lifted me up when I needed it and she never left me alone to wallow in my despair. She fought for me when I could no longer fight for myself. She had taken care of her father so many times, I knew how unfair this was for her. I prayed I could return to being the mother she once knew. She was my inspiration and my determination to never give up.

She's a born-again Christian and working on her singing career. The road to recovery is slow, but we lean on each other. I know Kristoff and Julian are looking over us and we'll never be without them. Julian often comes to us in a hummingbird, and Kristoff in a beautiful rainbow shining bright.

I look forward to the day I'll be a grandparent because I can't help but think that just maybe Julian will come back as her child and we'll all be together again.

My connection with nature has been a lifesaver for me. I'm grateful that I learned at an early age to appreciate the world around me. When I stand in the middle of a corn field or a lush valley, I realize there is something bigger than me. Every few months, I fly to Virginia and attend an institute where I meditate and recharge my soul.

This may sound corny to some people, but when I attend a retreat, I'm able to connect with my higher self. I let go of my ego and all of the tangible luxuries that go along with it. When I'm working, I get distracted with the things that don't really matter in life. But when I leave it behind for at least a week, I'm able to focus on my true self.

When I'm secluded in the world's natural environment, I meditate from the moment I wake up to the moment I go to sleep. It's imperative to have a clean system—no drugs, alcohol, or even caffeine, and it takes a lot of work and concentration to reach a higher consciousness. If I meditate deeply enough, I can reach Julian and Kristoff. It's exhilarating to know they're still with me. They're just not here on the plane that they once were.

For now, I'm working on transforming my anger into productivity. I've accepted that this is my life and I'm here for a greater purpose. I've learned a lot since the death of my son. I've learned a lot since the death of Kristoff. I continue to transform. I know I'm not afraid of dying but I'm also not trying to die.

There are things I want to do with my daughter, whom I'm grateful for in this life. I know it's a lot of pressure to place on her, but I don't know where I'd be without her. There are still places I want to explore and experience, and hopefully I will do it with the man I love. His name is Larry and he's a prominent cosmetic dentist for a lot of high-profile people, but you'd never know it because he's so humble.

My relationship with Larry has endured eight years of trials and tribulations. He has been my rock and I don't know how I would have survived any of this without him. On the night I first met him, he came to an art gallery where my son's work was being shown. He bought one of his pieces, and a pricey one too. My son was a no-show that night, but it was advertised that he would sign all purchased artwork. I told him I would have Julian sign the piece and personally bring it to his medical office in Beverly Hills.

After the event, he surprised me by helping me load all of Julian's pieces into my car, and then he took me to dinner. As nice as he was, I wasn't immediately drawn to him at first. We had opposing political views and he wasn't the type I was used to dating. I normally went out with athletes, but this was a welcomed change. Larry was smart, funny, caring, confident, and charismatic. By our third date I knew I could love him, but I never imagined eight years would go by and we'd still be together. He stood alongside me through the death of my son, the loss of my career, sobriety and, finally, Kristoff. It was a genuine love for each other that got us through, at times, a turbulent journey.

I didn't grow up knowing what a supportive and loving relationship looked like. I'm grateful for Larry having the patience to teach me. He has shown me what love looks like.

I am excited about the future. I am determined to help people find their purpose in life and show them it's worth fighting for. The journey is hard, but it's supposed to be so that we can feel the euphoria that comes with success. I'm finally reborn, but I realized that I had to go through a mountain of grief and tragedy to get here. In my son's honor, I opened a center called Stone Art, a nonprofit organization dedicated to helping people suffering from mental illness, addiction, and homelessness. I'm on a mission to spread the message of love and tolerance.

Today, I am sober. Every day is a miracle, which I do not take for granted. I was born to be who I am right now, not the fighter who trained for decades to beat the bloody hell out of someone. I was born to be something greater and far more significant. I give back to others every single day, even if it's as small as sitting and talking with someone for five minutes. I focus on my intent, I envision my goals and everything I want out of this life. My ego says that I'd rather have my son, but the universe didn't ask me. It's a hard pill to swallow, but I no longer scream and yell at an unknown God. I simply accept what is and move forward knowing that my journey was in motion before I was born. I know this life is a gift. And I'm committed to keep fighting for my life.

Mia's dad, Duncan, brought Mia's mom, Maria, from Mexico to the USA to start a family

Mia's mom and dad in the '60s

Little Mia and sister, Lesley, with their dad, Duncan

Mia

Mia's mom, Maria

Mia's college graduation from CSUN with a
bachelor's degree in Psychology

Kristoff and his biological
mom, who gave him
to an orphanage

Child actors of *Bad News Bears*

Kristoff, high-schooler by day, actor by night

Mia and proud
mom, Maria

Mia modeling in the '80s

Mia and Kristoff, '80s headshots

Mia and Kristoff in love

Mia and Kristoff tie the knot, 1991

Mia and Kristoff at son's funeral

Mia and Kristoff on the set of *The Talk*

Mia holding newborn son, Julian

Kristoff with firstborn, Julian

Julian's first boat ride

Mia with son, Julian, in Palm Springs home

Two-year-old old Julian loved by dad, Kristoff, and Nana, Ida Maria

Mia, Kristoff, and one-year-old Julian at Grandma's in Boise, ID, for the holidays

"Daughter Goes with Dad to Work" day at CBS television studios

Kristoff and Julian goofing around together

Proud artist Julian holding up a favorite, "The Real Manroe,"
one of his self-portraits inspired by one of his characteristics,
a mole in the same place as Marilyn Monroe

Julian and his
signature mole

Julian proudly posing next to his most popular art
piece, self-portrait, "Crucifix Dreamz"

Rare photo of Julian smiling for the camera

Mom visits Paris working at a vegan restaurant

Mia with daughter, Paris

Unbreakable brother/sister bond even within the
walls of a psychiatric hospital during visitation

Paris and Julian's last Christmas together, 2013

Julian's last Christmas

"I remember I use to be a karate kid...never thought I'd be smoking crack" - Julian St. John

"CruciFix Dreamz" My Pain is my Love/Shun'd By the herd like a Bird sent down from above/ I stay Lookin Up - JSJ

"I hope to find peace
Wherever I go I know one will be waiting
The day I begin
The day I wake up from this dream I'm in"
Julian St John

Rehab October 15, 2009 "I can't seem to get a grip on the day. It slowly fades. No one understands me" - Julian St. John

Deplete my Soul/ Greed Hate Power/ Empty Hopeless Gone/ Voids Deep - JSJ 2013

Top Left: Quote by son Julian who is like countless others who fall victim to addiction and mental illness

Top Right: Julian's Rehab Journal, 2009

2nd Picture (Left): Julian's self-portrait, "CruciFix Dreamz"

2nd Picture (Right): Julian sneaking cigarettes in the bathroom of the psychiatric hospital

Bottom Left: Julian at his debut art show. Poem is thought to have been inspired by his deep, inner longing to go "Home."

Mia training

Photo by Marty Solis

Mia defeats Christy Martin for the WBC title in 2012
Photo by Marty Solis

Mia with attorney, Mark Geragos

Mia and brother, David, in hometown, Boise, ID

Mia with sister, Lesley

Mia inducted into the Boxing Hall of Fame and supported
by sister, Lesley, and brother-in-law, Mike

Mia with boyfriend, Larry Rifkin

5745: Mia and Larry at home in Marina del Rey

Mia's photoshoot with pink gloves

Mia is a fighter by night, businesswoman by day

Mia taking in Joshua Tree

Mia wins the WBC Championship Belt

Mia wrapping hands

Christmas family photo with Mia, Kristoff, Paris, and Julian